O God,
If I Could
JUST BE HOLY

Kevin,

Every blessing to

you and your family —

Bob Dudek

O God, If I Could Just Be Holy
Living the Spirit-filled Life: Its Crisis and Process
Copyright © 2006 by Edward E. Dudek
Second Printing, 2006
ISBN-13: 978-0-9786686-1-7
ISBN-10: 0-9786686-1-8

All scripture quotations, unless otherwise noted, are taken from the Holy Bible: the Updated New American Standard version.

Printed in the United States of America.

O God, If I Could JUST BE Holy

Living the Spirit-filled Life:
Its Crisis and Process

EDWARD E. DUDEK

Contents

Acknowledgments

"I'm deeply indebted to a number of friends and students who read through the manuscript and offered very helpful suggestions. Many thanks, especially to Jeni Pedzinski, Laura Robertshaw, Sharon Canfield, Cherie Bowman, Jamie Swan and Michelle Winger who edited, and gave extra time and effort to the project."

Dedication

To the cherished memory of my parents, Betty and Abbie Dudek, who would have rejoiced with me regarding the publishing of this book. A special dedication to my dear wife, Milta, who has been by my side for more than 38 years.

Preface

I have had the privilege of presenting my Romans 6-8 Victorious Life Seminar in North America and around the world. The Lord has used it to transform lives and give hope to many who are struggling with their Christian walk.

I am inevitably asked if I have something in print that I can leave with people who take my seminar to help them grow in what they have learned. It has saddened me not to be able to give them something to help them in their steps towards maturity. This book is an answer to their requests and carefully lays out living the victorious Christian life that God desires them to have.

The names and places I refer to have been changed to protect privacy. I have used both genuine experiences and parables.

Even if you haven't taken the seminar, you will find this book very helpful in living the Christian life that God desires you to have.

Introduction

POSSIBILITY OR IMPOSSIBILITY?

The apostle Peter writes to his readers that they should be holy and godly people, but is that really possible? It is true that God commanded, "You shall be holy, for I am holy" (I Pe.1:14-16); but does He really expect us to be holy in ALL our behavior? Can our life really be similar to Paul's testimony, "The things you have learned and received and heard and seen in me, practice these things, and the God of peace will be with you"? (Phil.4:9) Or, should we simply expect, "The good that I want, I do not do, but I practice the very evil that I do not want"? (Rom.7:19)[1]

There is no doubt that Christ came to take away our sins. But did His work include giving us a pure heart here on earth, or is that the goal that we are supposed to strive for on our own? Is it possible—on this earth—to be spotless and blameless before God and man? Since God hates sin so much, does He want a born again believer to be an entirely new person in Christ who doesn't have to sin in thought, word, or deed every day? Or, maybe God wants a Christian to sin fairly regularly so that he or she will continue to depend upon Him. On the other hand, might God want a Christian's life to be so effective that he would not have to yield to temptation at all?[2]

Is there any evil that God cannot deliver us from when we are tempted? He must be able to deliver us from all evil—wouldn't you think? But are God's grace and sovereignty sufficient enough here on earth to really provide a way out when we are tempted so that we can always come through it victoriously? Or, should we expect our epitaph to be something like: "He was defeated by it, and enslaved to it"?[3]

Certainly, the purpose or result of our reconciliation to God by Christ's work on Calvary is that He can present us before God as holy, blameless, and free from any accusing charge. Without a doubt, God is able to guard and protect us from stumbling and to set us before Himself in heaven without blemish. But, will He keep us from falling at this moment, and the rest of today, and tomorrow and the day after? Will He enable us to live a practical, holy life on earth?[4]

Think about it. Have we always been pure-minded during times of affliction, distress, anguish, hardship, sleepless nights, hunger, or working to exhaustion? Have we always lived a life of integrity amid good and evil reports, amid slander or praise, or when we are unjustly accused? Is all of that our goal? After all, to what point can a person be kind and truthful when she is dishonored, experiences sorrow and grief, or is penniless? Is it possible to always be completely above reproach not only in the eyes of men, but also in God's sight?

Some may think that these questions are hinting at some kind of "perfectionism" where we won't be tempted anymore, or be able to sin. This is the farthest thing from my mind. I think these questions are simply the cry of a heart that hungers and thirsts for practical, everyday, down to earth righteousness and wants to know if it can be filled and satisfied.

Is it possible to live a life that is fully pleasing to the Lord every day? Read on to find the answer to that critical question.

REFERENCE NOTES TO INTRODUCTION

[1] II Pe.3:11.
[2] I Jn.3:5a; II Pe.3:14.
[3] cf. I Cor.10:13; cf. II Pe.2:19.
[4] Col.1:21-22; Jude 24.

Chapter 1

A Holy Life:
A Goal or a Reality?

As an eighteen year old in his first Olympics in 1984, Dan Jansen finished fourth in the 500-meter ice skating sprint. The bronze medallist beat him by only sixteen one hundredths of a second. He also finished sixteenth in the 1000 meter.[1]

At his second Olympics in Calgary, 1988, on the morning he was to skate the 500 meter sprint, Dan got a phone call from the United States. His twenty-seven-year-old sister, Jane, had been fighting leukemia for over a year, and she was dying. Dan spoke to her over the phone, but she was too sick to say anything in return. Their brother Mike had to relay Jane's message: She wanted Dan to race for her. However, before Dan skated that afternoon he received news that Jane had died. When he took to the ice, maybe he tried too hard for his sister. He slipped and fell on the first turn. He had never fallen before in a race. Four days later in the 1,000, he fell again, this time, of all places, on the straightaway.

How often is Dan's experience similar to that of our own Christian life? We know that we should be "obedient children of our heavenly Father" (cf. I Pe.1:14). We have great hope and expectancy that we can live a godly life. In fact, with Jesus' help we can be holy in every part of our lives, just like the Apostle Peter exhorts us to be.

After all, on the Cross, Jesus did bear our sins in His own body so that we might live for righteousness.[2]

Still, it doesn't take long for reality to set in. We fall on the ice, and later on, even on the straightaway. What is there left to do, then, but to train and discipline ourselves more? At his third Olympics in 1992, Dan Jansen was expected to win the 500 meters. For four years, he had been regarded as the best sprinter in the world and had already set world records. Unfortunately, he had trouble in the final turn and he finished fourth. In the 1,000 he tied for twenty-sixth. How often do we find ourselves in trouble "at a turn" and blow it once again? Perhaps it was never meant to be. Maybe living a consistent holy life is just a goal to seek after and not something to be attained here on earth.

At his fourth Olympics in 1994, Dan again was expected to win in the 500 meters, which was his specialty. Again tragedy struck. He didn't fall, but in the beginning of the final turn he fleetingly lost control on his left skate and put his hand down, slowing him just enough to finish in eighth place. Afterward, he apologized to his hometown of Milwaukee. Losing control…if we just had more control, then we could live that life that is consistently pleasing to the Lord.

Jansen had one race left, the 1,000 meters, and then he was going to retire. At the midway point of the race, the clock showed that he was skating at a world-record pace, and the crowd, including his wife and father, cheered. But with 200 meters to go, the hearts of the fans skipped a beat. Dan Jansen slipped. He didn't fall, but he slipped, touched his hand to the ice, regained control, and kept skating. When Dan crossed the finished line, he looked at the scoreboard and saw WR beside his name—world record. In his last race, Dan Jansen had finally won the gold medal. Maybe that's how the Christian life is supposed to be. You strive and you fall, then you work harder even though you experience defeat. Then finally, after many years and much effort, you begin to have a few more victories. And perhaps like Dan, we'll go out gloriously with a great victory over a certain temptation that has eluded us for most of our

Christian life. Or, if that doesn't work, at least we know that "when Christ appears we will be like Him because we shall see Him as He is" (I Jn.3:2).

But, what about the fact that "God's power has bestowed on each of us everything that pertains to life and godliness" (II Pe.1:3)? Peter says we have everything we need to live a life of godliness. So what's missing? Could it be something in our thinking or something that is lacking in our own personal life? Paul writes to the "holy and faithful brothers in Christ" (Col.1:2). Were they really holy in all manner of living? Or were they just like many of us: "in many things we all stumble" (Ja.3:2)?

Yet, in his epistle John says, "no one who is born of God sins" (I Jn.5:18a). In other words, it should be customary to not sin. The apostle isn't saying that a Christian cannot sin, but rather, that the usual, the normal is not to sin. No wonder, then, that Peter says we aren't supposed to "fashion ourselves" by the evil desires we used to have (I Pe.1:14). We don't have to. He says that we are to become holy in every aspect of our behavior—because we can. If we claim that we abide in Christ then we ought to be living as Jesus Himself lived.[3]

Oh, great! If living a holy life here on earth is both possible and is an obligation, now what are we supposed to do? Feel more self-condemned and depressed knowing that such a holy life is possible but not a reality? I guess so, UNLESS there is hope. The good news is that there is! Read on and discover that hope.

REFERENCE NOTES TO CHAPTER ONE

[1] Larson, Craig Brian, ed., *Contemporary Illustrations for Preachers, Teachers, & Writers*, Grand Rapids: Baker Books, 1996, pgs.119-20.
[2] I Pe.1:15-17; 2:14.
[3] cf. I Jn.3:6,9; cf. II Cor.6:16,18; 7:1; I Pe.1:15; I Jn.2:6.

Chapter 2

Beginning
at the Beginning

Dr. Marvin Overton is one of the finest brain surgeons in the United States. In 1992, he began attending a small church in Burnet, Texas, and received Christ as his personal Lord and Savior. Before his conversion he was a skeptic and rationalist who believed in the power of science. He was by his own description, cold-hearted. "I was a good surgeon," said Overton, "but I was coarse. I couldn't shed a tear. My attitude [toward patients] was tough."[1]

Due to the transformation God made in Overton's life, he now writes notes to them that contain encouraging quotes from Scripture, and he cares enough about patients to ask those scheduled for surgery, "If something goes wrong, are you comfortable that you know God and that you'll go to heaven?" Yikes!

Previous to Overton's conversion his god was wine. Not that he was an alcoholic; rather, he owned one of the finest wine collections in the country; over ten thousand bottles including every important vintage made between the late 1700s and 1930. His collection was valued at more than a million dollars. The Concord Jet flew French chefs and hand-carried bottles to the doctor's wine-tasting banquets. "Wine had become my idol," said Overton. "I worshipped the god Bacchus… I was an excellent heathen."

After his conversion, Overton sold his wine collection, giving much of the proceeds to charity.

Before his conversion, Overton was a Fort Worth socialite. Now he is one of the leaders in his small-town, blue-collar church in Burnet, Texas.

What has impressed people is his dramatic conversion. Michael McWhorter, chairman of the American Association of Neurological Surgeons science board has said, "Something changed his life." It's as if Marvin Overton died and a new Marvin Overton lives. Or, he formerly lived in darkness but now he walks in the light. None of this should surprise us.

The Scriptures tell us that **before we "came to Christ" we lived in sin and were under its power.** In fact, we were "criminals" who were dead in our trespasses, we didn't really know God, and we lived under His wrath because of our ungodliness and wrong-doing. But like Dr. Overton, God called us out of darkness into His marvelous light. He rescued and delivered us out of the dominion of darkness and transferred us into the kingdom of His Son. Christ ransomed us from the curse pronounced by the Law. Our sins were also forgiven on account of Jesus and for His sake. He has accepted us and taken us into His favor in the person of His beloved Son. Wonderful! [2]

But, there's more! **We have been reconciled to God.** We are now citizens of heaven and members of God's family. Death can't hold us. God has blessed us in Christ with every spiritual blessing in the heavenly places. And we have a perfect inheritance reserved in heaven for us. What more could we want?! But, there is more! [3]

Because of God's great mercy He caused us to become "regenerated" or "spiritually reborn". And, we are called His children because we've been "born again". He gave us life. Besides that—and here's where it can seem unbelievable—because you were united to Christ **you have become a new person altogether. Your past—**

your old life—is *gone*. The person you used to be has passed away. A new life has begun.[4]

But you may be thinking, **"How can this be? In part I am a new person but I'm also a lot like the old one."** That may be. But, we need to begin to see what God actually did at our conversion. God imparted His life into us. We became spiritually reborn with a complete change of life. God is not interested in improving our old life, self or nature; His work brings about such a change that we are truly a new creation of His, in Christ—a new being, created in the likeness of God in righteousness and holiness. God has no desire for us to have a sinful life; He wants us to be genuinely pure and holy.[5]

For Personal Reflection/Group Discussion:

1. This chapter wouldn't be complete unless we ask ourselves a few important questions. (Please write out/discuss your answer for each question):

    a. Do you know beyond a shadow of a doubt that you have confessed and forsaken every one of the sins that God has shown you? Has He fully forgiven them? On what do you base your certainty of the forgiveness of your sins? Reflect on I Jn.1:9; Prov.28:13; II Cor.7:8-11; Col.1:14.

    b. Are you absolutely sure that you have fully entrusted yourself to and have confidence only in Jesus Christ and His work on Calvary for salvation, and not in anyone or anything else? How does your daily life show or not show this?

    c. Are you completely sure that you have been "born again"? If your answer is "yes," how can you be so sure that you have been "born from above"? If you were to die right now and stand before God, who then asks you why He should let you into heaven, what would you specifically say to Him? Read and reflect on John 3:4-8; 1:12-13; II Cor.5:17.

d. What concrete evidence do you have that proves to both God and to man that you have been made a "new creation" in Christ? Read and reflect on I Jn.2:29; 4:7. Have you made things right with others and also made restitution where necessary? Read and reflect on Ezek.33:14-16 & Lk.19:8-9.

2. Write a poem, a song or a prayer that captures the essence of your relationship with Jesus Christ as your Savior and Lord.

If you have any doubts regarding any of the above questions, or would like to discuss any of your answers, please feel free to call 1-800-323-3417 (Bethany College of Missions).

REFERENCE NOTES TO CHAPTER TWO

[1] Larson, Craig Brian, ed., *Contemporary Illustrations for Preachers, Teachers, & Writers*, Grand Rapids: Baker Books, 1996, pgs. 35-36

[2] Col.3:7; Rom.3:9; Col.2:13; Gal.4:8; Jn.3:36; cf. Rom.1:18; I Pe.2:9; Col.1:13; Gal.3:13; I Jn.2:12; Eph.1:6.

[3] Rom.5:10; Phil.3:20; Eph.2:19; Heb.2:14; Eph.1:3; I Pe1:4.

[4] I Pe.1:23,25; I Jn.3:1; cf. Gal.4:8-9; I Pe.1:3; Col.2:13; II Cor.5:17.

[5] II Cor.5:18; Eph.4:24; I Thes.4:3,7.

Chapter 3

Dead to Sin?

In 1847, a certain man owned a farm in California. He heard that gold had been discovered in the southern part of the state. So, he sold his farm to a Colonel Sutter and headed south.

The Colonel built a dam in the stream that passed through his farm. One day his little daughter brought some sand that she had picked up near the dam. As she was letting the sand pass through her fingers a visitor saw the brilliance of gold in the sand. This was the first genuine gold discovered in California.

The first owner wanted gold and was willing to go anywhere to get it. Yet $38,000,000 worth of gold was eventually found on that farm where he had lived! How far are we willing to go and what are we willing to do to "find the gold" and the answers to the problems we have in our Christian walk? Unfortunately, many of us are not willing to go wherever necessary to have a walk with the Lord that is pleasing in His sight. Unfortunate? Yes, because the "gold" is —within us. What "gold"? Read on.

Craig, a young homosexual, was converted to Christ and was living a fulfilling life, until he began to fall back into homosexual acts. He cried, pleaded with the Lord, and kept finding temporary relief from his sin. He was doing all he could to stay free and live a life that was pleasing to the Lord. He would experience one or two victories only to taste defeat at the next turn. Finally, "gold" was discovered. He writes: "I couldn't see it before. Now I understand. Christ had broken the powers of homosexuality at the Cross. My Jesus had been so small and the benefits of the Cross so insignificant. I had been judging myself by how I felt, not by who I was in Him... I had been reinforcing homosexuality for years by my neurotic, whining, faithless prayer that pleaded for a deliverance that was already provided... I knew now that I could ultimately walk free."

Galatians 2:20 had been the liberating truth for him: "I have been crucified with Christ; and it is no longer I who live, but Christ lives in me; and the life which I now live in the flesh I live by faith in the Son of God, who loved me and gave Himself up for me". He saw that in some marvelous way, the old Craig had been crucified with Christ and that homosexual had died with Him. Craig already knew that Christ lived in him but now he also understood that the life he was to live was to be lived by complete dependence upon Christ and total confidence in what He had done for him on Calvary.

How is this possible? How can a person who is sexually immoral, or is greedy, envious or selfishly ambitious or a slanderer, thief, or drunk—anyone for that matter—be genuinely transformed like Craig? Certainly not by one's own strength or wisdom. It has to do with what Christ accomplished on Calvary's cross and with God's ability to really change a life. This chapter will help explain these two issues.

Saul at one time was a blasphemer, a persecutor and a violent aggressor. But all things are possible for God. Nothing is too difficult for Him. Saul the enslaved, independent Pharisee was transformed into the Apostle Paul, who years later wrote Romans chapter 6 that explains the basis for his change and the change that anyone can experience in Christ.[1]

"Where sin increased, grace abounded much more" (Rom.5:20). So, "are we to continue to live in sin so that grace may increase" (6:1)? In other words, is it morally acceptable to continue a relationship with sin as if it were your master? Absolutely not! And then notice the apostle's question: "How shall we who died to sin still live in it" (v.2b)? Not, how shall we who are dead by reason of our sins, but rather how shall we who died with regards to sin, still live in it? How shall we who were separated from sin as master, ending our relationship with its enslaving power, continue in a relationship with it?

My dad passed away in July of 2003. As I saw him in the casket, I couldn't help but think that he really wasn't there. Oh, his body was there, but Dad had been separated from his body and was now with Jesus in heaven. Death means separation. Dad became separated from his family and this world in a moment. In a real sense, he had died to this world.

Being "dead to sin" in Romans 6 means to be separated from sin as master, to be detached from its enslavement. It does not mean that we can't be tempted anymore, as if we've become insensitive to sin's power or its enticement. And it certainly does not mean that we can never sin, being in some way immune to that possibility. But Paul does make it clear that whatever our relationship was to sin as an enslaving master before we were saved, that relationship has been terminated. The Apostle in this chapter is stating what happened the moment Christ entered your life. Whether we were aware of it or not, it happened. Remember Craig? Sin is not meant to be your master. You are no longer under its control.

Paul in Rom.6:6a states: "Knowing this, that our old self was crucified with Him." God dealt with the person we once were—that unregenerate Dave, Don, Susan, Marsha. "I have been crucified with Christ" (Gal.2:20). The depraved person we all were, with our desires, thoughts, passions and experiences, has been nailed to the Cross with Christ. You, who lived under the condemnation and enslavement of sin, died with Christ on the Cross. God has identified us with Christ's crucifixion. That is the way He sees it. Notice the important results of our joint-crucifixion with Christ.

- One result of being crucified with Christ is that the sinful body is done away with. This "body of sin" that Paul is referring to is the human, physical, sinful body that is under sin's dominion. Our "unredeemed body" ceased to be such an instrument of sin. Even though the body is still weak, mortal and perishable, it is now a "member of Christ" and is a "temple of the Holy Spirit".[2]

- The second result of being identified with Christ in His crucifixion is that from now on we don't have to be a slave to sin. This result isn't based upon our determination or self-effort. We do not have to be a slave to sin as master anymore because we are crucified with Christ. God does not free us from sin's dominion by strengthening the person we were before we came to Christ, but by crucifying him.[3]

Only What Jesus Could Do

Suffering a severe defeat at the hands of the Edomites, King David tells the Lord, "O give us help against the adversary, for deliverance by man is in vain. Through God we shall do valiantly, and it is He who will tread down our adversaries" (Ps.60:11-12). When we try to live a Christian life that is constantly pleasing to the Lord, it doesn't take long to realize that the help that mere man can give is worthless, and that it's only through God that we can fight victoriously. Only He can bring about that victory.

Death no longer has dominion over Christ. When Jesus hung on Calvary's Cross Death reigned and had power over Him. When He died and was resurrected, death did not exercise such lordship over him anymore. And not just that. As Paul states in Rom.6:10, by the death that Jesus died, He died to sin, that is, He once and for all ended His relation to sin as master. Jesus never sinned—ever, but He did give Himself up as an offering for our sins and bore them on the Cross. He was truly our Substitute and Representative. Since Jesus died in our place and represented us on Calvary, Paul tells us in Romans 6 that sin had a claim on Him. That is, sin reigned as master over the world's Substitute and Representative. Notice that whatever the relationship was between Christ on Calvary and sin as an enslaving power, that relation was completely ended once for all when He died. And now, the life that our Lord lives, He lives in uninterrupted fellowship with His heavenly Father.[4]

Only What We Can Do

So what does this really have to do with us? "In the same way" [i.e., "so" or "likewise"] "count yourselves dead to sin but alive to God in Christ Jesus" (Rom.6:11, NIV). Notice, Jesus did what He had to do: die to sin once and for all. Now we must do what is our responsibility: to consider ourselves as having ended our relation to sin as master. Because we are in Christ, we are to look upon ourselves as having died to sin once and for all!

At conversion, we were freed from sin and its enslavement. We are not in the process of dying but rather we have already died and been separated from sin as an enslaving power. Thus, we are in this permanent condition because of the one-time decisive event of Christ dying to sin. This is what is true about each believer and what is 'real,' whether we know it, feel it, or understand it. However, having come to know that truth, Paul says, "You must now regard yourself as dead to sin; consider yourself as having ended once and for all your relation to sin as master."

This is not "playing pretend". Christ's death has really severed our relationship to sin as master. We must continually count on the fact that we are truly and finally separated from sin as an enslaving power and that we are also really alive to God through our union with Jesus Christ—because it is true!

Jed was all excited about the truth that he had discovered regarding his identification with Christ. He understood that Jesus had "died to sin" on Calvary's Cross, and that he too—Jed—had been separated from sin as an enslaving power in his own life. Then he began to think about whether or not this would really "work" in his own life. "How much do I have to believe before it will become really true in my life? What about my weaknesses and previous failures at trying to live the Christian life? How strong do I need to become so that I can die to sin and live unto God? How sincere do I really need to be so that I can become separated from sin as an enslaving power? If I can just consider myself dead to sin, then maybe that will make it happen. Or if I could at least feel as if I were dead to sin, then maybe it would all become true. What if God made my life holy first? Then I could believe that I died to sin and that I am alive unto Him. I'm depressed and confused. O God, please help me!"

God does not want us to believe or count on anything that is not true. In regards to our relationship to sin as master, seeing what happened to Christ on Calvary is the key. On the Cross, Jesus, was separated once and for all from sin as an enslaving power. When we enter into union with Christ (at salvation), we become separated from sin as master at that instant. Why? Because what happened to Christ on Calvary, God also caused to happen to us—freedom from sin's dominion—whether we knew it at the time of salvation or not.

Frank knew that he was a born-again believer. Yet, he always saw God as a judge and ruler. One Sunday the minister was speaking from Galatians about sonship. The pastor read, "Because you are sons, God has sent forth the Spirit of His Son into our hearts, crying, 'Abba! Father!' Therefore you are no longer a slave, but a son; and if a son, then an heir through God" (Gal. 4:6-7). It was as if a light went on. All of a sudden Frank realized that he was a son of God and that God was his heavenly Father. It was transforming. His prayer life and general outlook changed in the days ahead. When had Frank become a son? Was it during those glorious days or at the time of his conversion? It was when he had been saved.

The same is true regarding our identification with Christ. At the moment of salvation, every Christian is entirely separated from sin as master. Granted, most Christians are not aware of this since they are thinking primarily of the forgiveness of sins and coming into a relationship with Jesus. But the fact is, you and I died to sin once and for all the moment we were born again, independent of what we knew, felt, or thought about this occurrence.

Like Frank who embraced the truth regarding his sonship, we need to embrace the truth regarding our identification with Christ, i.e., that we truly and genuinely are dead to sin—completely separated from sin as master—and that we are alive unto God, able to live in uninterrupted communion with Him. God considers us as such, and so should we. Our identification with Christ in His death and resurrection is not some duty to work out, but rather a privilege to take hold of. "So let it be with you—regard yourselves as dead to sin, but as living for God through union with Christ Jesus" (Rom.6:11, TCNT).

Is All of This That Important?

Does all of this really make that much difference? What if we consciously count ourselves dead to sin and alive to God? Is it that important? It most certainly is! One implication is that we don't ever have to let sin dominate and reign again in our bodies.[5]

Glenn was a Christian man who loved to eat. One could probably say that in many ways he lived to eat. Wherever he was, at whatever time of the day, Glenn was looking for his next snack or meal. He was a glutton, and the craving to eat to excess was his master. Before, as well as after his conversion, Glenn had tried everything to gain control over this lord; he denied that he even had such a master, he tried to kill it by yelling at it and cursing it, and he just tried plain ol' will power to stifle it. Such attempts worked for a little while but all ultimately ended with defeat. There certainly was a master who was controlling him and prevailing over his body.

Fortunately, this is not the end of the story. Glenn discovered that this gluttonous man had died with Christ when he was saved. The Apostle Paul's testimony had become Glenn's testimony as well, "I have been crucified with Christ; and it is no longer I who live, but Christ lives in me; and the life which I now live in the flesh I live by faith in the Son of God, who loved me and gave Himself for me" (Gal.2:20). Glenn also came to know that he had ended his relationship with the master who was exercising authority over him. With this in view, he presented himself to God as one who was "alive from the dead". He was now daily counting on the fact that at Calvary, Christ had effectively and genuinely dealt with his former master. Glenn realized that he didn't have to continue to let this master reign over his body anymore. No more did he have to put his body at the disposal of this enslaving craving. I'm not telling this parable to give the impression that Glenn didn't have any more struggles with his eating, but rather to emphasize that such masters must first and foremost be dealt with at the Cross.

One of the biblical principles Glenn used in his pursuit of victory was to make a full surrender to God. Notice *when* he did this—and *how*. Glenn presented himself to God as one who was "alive from the dead" (Rom.6:13). It was only after he knew that he was crucified with Christ and that he had died to sin as an enslaving power in his life that Glenn made this full surrender to the Lord. He was truly a living sacrifice, holy and acceptable to God.[6]

In reality, Glenn had been yielding his body to sin as master. Now realizing his identification with Christ in His resurrection, Glenn saw that he could serve the Lord in faith and love. There was no way he had to continue presenting any part of his body to sin to be used as an "instrument or tool" for gluttony. He put himself in God's hands to use his members as instruments for doing what was right. So, the apostle Paul's word to us is, "As you formerly presented your members as slaves to uncleanness and ever increasing iniquity, so now present your members to righteousness that leads to holiness" (Rom.6:19).[7]

It is true that one's body makes a terrible master. Like a prizefighter, the body needs to be put under strict discipline and be directed for useful service. The apostle made his body obey him. However, this daily "exercise" must be preceded by offering our bodies as a sacrifice—alive, holy, and acceptable to God. When

Isaac presented himself on the altar at the request of Abraham, he was truly a living sacrifice and had set himself apart for God's purpose. God doesn't take such surrender lightly. In fact, He is "tremendously pleased." Paul writes to the Corinthian church, "you have been bought with a price: therefore, glorify God with your body" (I Cor.6:20).

For Personal Reflection/Group Discussion:

1. In light of the rest of chapter 6 of Romans, explain in simple terms what the apostle meant when he asked, "How shall we who died to sin still live in it?" (Rom.6:2b).

2. If a person is already a Christian why can he or she *not* "die to sin" as an enslaving master? (Hint: What happened at conversion? See Rom.6:1-2,11).

3. Have you confessed and renounced any sin(s) that the Holy Spirit has revealed to you? (You can also look at the list of sins at the end of Chapter 7). Confessing and forsaking sin is important in order to take the steps in Question #4.

4. Have you taken these three simple steps that Paul outlines for us in Romans chapter 6?

    a. KNOW—meditate on the "knowing" in Rom.6:5-6 by actively reflecting on what the Apostle is writing to his readers.

    b. CONSIDER YOURSELF—count on and embrace the facts that you have died to sin and that you are alive unto God in Christ (Rom.6:11).

    c. SURRENDER YOURSELF FULLY—to God as one who is alive from the dead (Rom.6:13,19; 12:1)

REFERENCE NOTES TO CHAPTER THREE

[1] I Tim.1:13; Mt.19:26; Jer.32:27
[2] cf. Rm 6:12-13,19; I Cor.15:42-44, I Cor.6:15, 19.
[3] Rom.6:6c.
[4] Gal.1:4; II Cor.5:21; Heb.10:12,26; 9:28.
[5] cf. Rom.6:12-13.
[6] Rom.12:1.
[7] cf. Rom.6:13.
[8] I Cor.9:27; Rom.12:1.

Chapter 4

If Good Experiences Would Only Last

Robert was a sincere Christian who had discovered the truths of Romans 6. It was truly life transforming for him. There was an 'ease' in his walk with the Lord. He had a freedom to be the person God wanted him to be that he had never experienced previously.

However, as those glorious days passed into weeks, something happened. Robert responded to someone in an angry manner and he sensed right away that he had sinned. He confessed and forsook it and received the Lord's forgiveness. But those feelings of ease and freedom didn't return. In fact, he found himself committing sin in a few other areas within a short period of time. He was worried. He began to doubt that anything had truly happened when he had embraced the truths of his identification with Christ. He prayed again with more vigor but he kept falling back into sin.

Robert thought that perhaps he wasn't being sincere enough in his praying. So he began to pray more earnestly about his life, family, church and friends. He surrendered himself again to the Lord. That helped, for a little while. When he told someone of his difficulties the person said that he needed to read his Bible more and to spend more time with the Lord. That made sense. So, he began reading the Scriptures, reflecting on them and asking the Lord to speak to him. He had some wonderful times and experiences, but it only lasted for a while.

Then Robert began to feel more desperate. A friend told him that he should be fasting and offering thanksgiving and praise to the Lord for all that He had already done for him. So Robert began to fast twice a week since he wanted so much to return to the same feelings that he had before. He wanted to experience the satisfaction of once again pleasing the Lord in everything that he did. During these periods of fasting, he searched his heart, was sincere before the Lord, and began reading good Christian books, and it all worked— for a while.

Then Robert began to attend more church services and conferences. He gave more than his tithe to the church and mission outreaches. He started to evangelize with a church group once a week. He even began to dress differently to see if that would help him in his dilemma. It was to no avail. The more he tried to do good things, the more he found himself doing the opposite. He began to feel genuinely miserable and exhausted from everything he was trying to do to live a holy life.

He felt like a walking civil war. Oh, he had his good days, but nothing like he had experienced before, and these good days were relatively short-lived. He didn't feel spiritual at all; in fact, at times he felt more like he did when he wasn't converted.

Whatever he tried to do to better the situation, it only seemed to work for a little while. It got to the point where he didn't even understand his own actions at times. He loved God's Word and wanted to obey it, but so often he ended up doing the very thing he hated. It was almost as if sin as master was doing these things instead of him, but he knew that wasn't really true. Robert had finally had it. He wanted so much to be conformed to the image of Christ and had done everything he and others could think of to "get him back on track." Someone finally told him, "Robert, this is just the way the Christian life is." O' what a miserable life!

What had happened? Simply, Robert had put himself "under the law." That's right. He had gotten to the point where he was putting his eyes and efforts on techniques and obligations instead of keeping his faith in Christ's work and ability. The law cannot deliver anyone from sin's power.

Being "under the law" means to be controlled and governed by the law's obligations. When a person tries to use the law to become righteous, he places himself under the law. This is very clear at salvation—coming to Christ means that you are not counting on being saved by being good enough or by obeying God's laws.[1] Living a holy and righteous life doesn't come simply by obeying laws and being disciplined.

Unfortunately, that truth seems to get blurry at times for many Christians when they try to live out their Christian life. The following are two testimonies from Christians who attended my Victorious Life Seminar:

> "I have come to know that the Christian life is not a list of 'do's' and 'don'ts' but faith through Jesus Christ our Lord."—Phillip from Ghana.

> "I have been making rules and breaking them, but these lessons have caused me to know that this will never work. I need to live under the control of the Holy Spirit."—John from Kenya.

There is nothing wrong with God's law. It reveals His will; it's impartial; it requires obedience and forbids what is wrong (Rom.7:12). Yet, although it does demand righteousness, it can't make a person righteous.[2]

Joan became convicted of coveting through reading God's word. She now had a decision to make. She confessed and renounced coveting and received forgiveness. But then Joan began to think that in order to maintain her right relationship with God, she needed to begin depending on doing what this command required. Now she was in trouble. Why? Because, instead of seeking and depending upon the righteousness that comes from God through faith in Christ, she turned inward. She sought to depend on the law to get her back to God and to make her holy as God requires. This is where sin as master finds its opportunity. It ended up producing in Joan all kinds of wrong desires. Resting our holiness or right standing with God on obedience to the law leads to defeat. The law or our formulas can never bring us to maturity. In fact, when a person is under the law, the Holy Spirit isn't even doing the leading. You desert God's grace when you try to be righteous through the law, and this leads to bondage. Both Joan and Robert discovered this.[3]

How often do Christians seem to find two laws or principles working inside of them? On one hand, evil is there and ready. It's as if sin is the master and has control of the person's tongue or other bodily member. Then, there's the other governing principle, a different one: it's the wanting and desiring to do what the law requires. It's not that he doesn't delight in or agree with God's law, he does, but he finds these two opposing principles at work in him. Plain and simple, he wants to do right but doesn't seem to find the power or ability to do it. How many Christians do you think have experienced just that? In fact how many would admit that they have felt like a prisoner? Perhaps worse yet, they were just plain miserable because of this constant inward battle.

Is this really the best that anyone can expect—"under the law"? Yes it is, with his mind he will continue to serve the Lord and he will continue to "will to do" the good because he sincerely wants to do it. But the doing of the good—that's the problem. It's not like he never does anything good. Yet he desires a deliverance from his inner civil war. Stronger resolutions and more sincere motives just don't do it. Oh, it might better the situation for awhile, but "woe is me...I'm done for." Have you ever felt like that?

The Answer

Is there an answer to this, or should we accept the testimony of Robert's friend, "We all have and are walking civil wars. That's just the way the Christian life is"? Well, thankfully the Lord doesn't see it that "way". And once again, Christ's work on Calvary provides the answer.

You know, the law—the Ten Commandments, for example— only applies to the living. It certainly wouldn't have any authority or jurisdiction over a person who is dead. Suppose, for example, a husband dies while he and his wife are married. She would then have the liberty to marry another man if and when she chose to do so. But it was because of the death of her husband that the wife became free or separated from the marriage contract and wasn't under its authority anymore.

Now suppose that while her first husband was alive, she just decided to marry another man. This would not only make her legally a bigamist but according to God's law she would also be considered an adulteress.

Notice, in the first situation, because of the death of her husband, the woman was no longer under the marriage law's obligation and she was free to marry another. In other words, the law that joined her to her husband no longer bound her. The marriage law still existed, but she was released from it because of the death of another, that is, her husband.

So what's the point? Well, it's this marriage situation that Paul uses to explain the Christian's relationship to the law: "It's the same in your case, my brothers. The crucified body of Christ made you dead to the Law" (Rom.7:4a, Moffatt). In other words, as the wife was freed from the law by the death of her husband, so also, we were freed from the Law by the death of Christ. When Christ died, God put us to death in regards to the Law. At salvation we were released from the Law that had bound us. There is no more need to try to "serve God in the old obedience to the letter of the Law".[4]

Amazingly there's more! At salvation we were also joined to the risen Christ so that we might bear fruit for God" (Rom.7:4b)!

How glorious!! So, instead of serving the obsolete letter of the law, we "serve in a new way, in the Spirit" (v.6, Phillips). This is what Robert was searching for at the beginning of the chapter but couldn't find. It's because he was looking in the wrong place. It has to do with our identification with Christ; because Jesus died to sin AND to the Law, so have we. Those truths need to be embraced so that we can truly live and experience God's grace to its fullest.

Perhaps this sounds too 'theoretical' or 'doctrinal.' We need to know the truth because the truth sets us free. But read on, because chapter 5 is key.

For Personal Reflection/Group Discussion:

1. Why was Robert seeking help and trying one idea after another? What did he experience?

2. What does it mean to be "under the law"? Describe the experience of it.

3. Reflect/discuss Romans 7:1-6 and its practical implications.

REFERENCE NOTES TO CHAPTER FOUR

[1] Phil.3:9; Taylor.
[2] Gal.2:16,19; Phil.3:9
[3] Cf. Heb.7:19; ct. Gal.5:18; Gal.5:4.
[4] Rom.7:1-4; v.6; Phillips.

Chapter 5

"Oh, the Spirit of Grace!"

We still have choices to make. We need to choose to walk in the Spirit. We still need to choose to believe that our flesh has been crucified. We need to stand fast in our liberty.[1] "Now this is our boast," Paul writes to the Corinthians, "our conscience testifies that we have conducted ourselves in the world, and especially in our relations with you, in the holiness and sincerity that are from God. We have done so not according to worldly wisdom but according to God's grace" (II Cor. 1:12, NIV).

In the *Discipleship Journal*, editor Susan Maycinik writes, "The line between obedience and performance can be a blurry one. Yet it is an important distinction to grasp, because obedience leads to life, and performance to death." The following are a few of her distinctions. As you read them, notice that they could be placed respectively "under grace" and "under the law":[2]

"Obedience is seeking God with your whole heart. Performance is having a quiet time because you feel guilty if you don't."

"Obedience is finding ways to let the Word of God dwell in you richly. Performance is quickly scanning a passage so you can check it off your Bible reading plan."

"Obedience is inviting guests to your home for dinner. Performance is feeling anxious about whether every detail of the meal will be perfect."

"Obedience is following the promptings of God's Spirit. Performance is following a list of man-made requirements."

Being "under grace" involves living by faith and following the guidance of the Holy Spirit. There is freedom in living according to God's grace. Not the liberty of license, but freedom to serve others in love. Faith finds its expression in love.[3]

In *Moody* magazine, pastor and author Leith Anderson writes:[4]

"Charleen [my wife] and I grew up together and dated through high school and college. We've been married for most of our lives, but we've never drafted a list of rules for our lives together. Don't misunderstand, we are both committed to Jesus Christ as Lord and to the Holy Spirit as our guide. We hold God's moral law in highest value—truth, morality, honesty, honoring of parents, and preserving life.

"When we first married, we could not have anticipated all that would be included in 'better and worse, richer and poorer, sickness and health.' There is no way that any set of rules or any book on marriage could have told us what to do. We've based our decisions on a relationship of commitment, love, and growing to know each other better every day.

"That's the way the Christian life is to be lived—by relationship, not rules. The Christian's relationship with God is based on love and commitment, holding God's moral law in highest regard but depending on the grace of

God to live out His morality in everyday circumstances. Every relationship is a bit different, so there is freedom. Every relationship learns and grows through experience. Life by the Spirit, not by the rules."

The Holy Spirit is the key to living the Christian life. We know that we have died to the law and to sin as master. We also know that we should try to live 'under grace', but how? Yes, our God is a gracious God who gives favor and grace to the undeserving. Still, how do we live a life of obedience that is pleasing to Him? We've already seen that the law doesn't give us any ability to live such a life.

Notice what the apostle says in Rom.8:2-4, "For the law of the Spirit of life in Christ Jesus has set you free from the law of sin and of death. For what the Law could not do, weak as it was through the flesh, God did: sending His own Son in the likeness of sinful flesh and as an offering for sin, He condemned sin in the flesh, so that the righteous requirement of the Law might be fulfilled in us, who do not walk according to the flesh but according to the Spirit."

In 1863, the President of the United States, Abraham Lincoln, issued the Emancipation Proclamation and set all the slaves in the southern states free. Yet despite his edict, the slaves remained slaves. Even though they were legally (positionally) free, they were unable to take advantage of their deliverance. It wasn't until the northern army under General Sherman came and overwhelmed the southern forces that the slaves were actually physically set free. They had been legally free for five years, but not until the superior forces of the northern army came were they truly set free.

Remember how the law or principle of sin that has warred against our mind eventually made us prisoners? The Law didn't have the capability to deal effectively with the power of sin in our lives. We were seeking deliverance, but the Law and our formulas weren't accomplishing it. Thankfully there is a higher principle—"a superior force" than that of sin as master! It's the Holy Spirit, who is the Giver of Life. He is the One who delivers us from the rule and power of sin because of Christ's work on Calvary. Also, notice the result of His work: "that the requirement of the Law might be fulfilled in us who don't walk according to the flesh but according to the Spirit" (Rom.8:3). In other words, God's Spirit can now fulfill in us what the Law requires. Previously, we knew that we were supposed to be free but we weren't living out that freedom. Now, as we walk by the Spirit, loving God with our whole being and loving our neighbor as ourselves actually happens in daily life.

What does all of this mean? Since you are identified with Christ in His death and resurrection, your relationship to sin as master and to the jurisdiction of the law in your life has been terminated. It is the Holy Spirit who can and wants to empower you to live a holy life.

So, Where Do You Start? "Be Filled with the Spirit."

Robert Kircher writes: "As you leave the whole burden of your sin, and rest upon the atoning work of Christ, so leave the whole burden of your life and service, and rest upon the present inworking of the Holy Spirit.

"Give yourself up, morning by morning, to be led by the Holy Spirit, and go forward praising and at rest, leaving Him to manage you and your day. Cultivate the habit, all through the day of joyfully depending upon and obeying Him, expecting Him to guide, to enlighten, to reprove, to teach, to use, and to do in and with you what He will. Count upon His working as a fact, altogether apart from sight or feeling.

"Only let us believe in and obey the Holy Spirit as RULER of our lives, and cease from the burden of trying to manage ourselves, then shall the fruit of the Spirit—love, joy, peace, longsuffering, kindness, goodness, faithfulness, meekness, self-control—appear in us, as He will, to the glory of God." [5]

40

The apostle Paul in the fifth chapter of Ephesians told his readers to take great care in how they lived. He didn't want them to act thoughtlessly but rather to know what the Lord's will was for them in their daily living. He wanted them to "be filled with the Spirit" (Eph.5:18)!

What is interesting in this text is what Paul says in the original Greek language. He gives a command to his Christian readers: be filled with the Spirit! He wasn't giving them an idea or an option to think about; he tells them that they must be filled with the Spirit. His command is in the plural, which means that being filled with the Spirit is for everyone, and not just for a select few within the church. His order is also given in the present continuous tense, which means that being filled should be an ongoing process and not something that you experience once and then "you have it or do it." It's something that is to be experienced moment-by-moment in a Christian's life.

But what does this important command mean? In other words, what is it to be continuously filled with the Spirit? Perhaps if we look at a different context, we can see what Paul is referring to here in Ephesians. What does it mean, for example, to be "filled with" all kinds of sin? It would mean that person is full of unrighteousness and overflows with it. For example, he may revel in every kind of wrongdoing and be versed in every kind of ill will. His life would be characterized by what filled it: unrighteousness, depravity, covetousness, greed, envy, or pride.[6]

On the other hand, someone "filled with" wisdom, compassion or encouragement would mean that person has wisdom in his life or shows compassion to others or is encouraging those around him. And a Christian who is "filled with" the Holy Spirit is one who has the fruit of the Spirit overflowing in his or her life. Their Christian walk is characterized by love, joy, peace, patience, kindness, goodness, faithfulness, gentleness and self-control; like Dorcas who was "full of good works." Here was a Christian woman who "was abounding with deeds of kindness and charity which she continually did" (Acts 9:36). She was bubbling over with much kindness.[7]

Are you full of God's Spirit? Is your life a continual reflection of Jesus' life? Or, do you have to admit that your life is characterized more by some of the things that Paul warned his Ephesian readers about: unwholesome words, bitterness, anger, malice, impurity, covetousness, greed, shameful conduct, or suggestive jesting that isn't befitting for a child of God? If sins such as these or others do not control or characterize your life, do you have godly qualities that do? Does your life really demonstrate, as Paul exhorts his readers, only edifying words that help others according to the need of the moment, generosity, being tenderly affectionate, always forgiving others, following Christ's example in living a life of love, being true and good? In fact, the apostle further says that the result of one who is continually filled with the Spirit is "speaking to one another in psalms and hymns and spiritual songs." There is "singing and making melody with your heart to the Lord." Furthermore, he is "always giving thanks for all things in the name of our Lord Jesus Christ to God even the Father." And he is subject to others "in the fear of Christ" (Eph.5:19-21).

So the crucial question is, "Are you continually filled with the Spirit?". Is He the One who is in control of your life and demonstrates the life of Jesus through you in a consistent manner? If we are filled with the Spirit then we should not only have the conviction that we are, but our life should also show it. Or, perhaps you readily admit that you are not full of God's Spirit. If you are not, take heart, because you can be.

How? How can we obey God's command to be filled with the Spirit? It doesn't come about through blind hope, or trying to be more spiritual, or by using a formula to cause it to happen. You can even insist on doing it your way. You could wrongfully arrive at the conclusion: "God knows I'm here, He can fill me when He so chooses."

If you are not sure that you are filled with the Spirit because your life really doesn't show it "that much," take heart because you can be filled and controlled by the Holy Spirit—right now. Paul's expressed command in Eph.5:18 is in the passive voice that simply means that you can't fill yourself—someone else has to do it. Remember when you came to Christ? Jesus came into your heart and life because you invited Him to come in. It's the same with the Holy Spirit. Yes, you already have the Spirit of God; if you didn't have the Spirit of Christ (another name for the Holy Spirit) you wouldn't belong to the Lord.[8] Even so, Paul would not be commanding Christians, who already had the Holy Spirit, to be filled with Him if it were just automatic without a choice. If it were not possible to be filled and if it did not have great significance in a Christian's life, Paul would not have mentioned it.

We receive the filling of the Spirit through faith. That's it. No magic formulas or rites. A simple prayer would be, "Lord Jesus, I open my heart to You. In obedience to the command I ask You, Jesus, to fill me with the Holy Spirit. Do this so that I may at least begin now to have a life that is always full of the Spirit and controlled by Him. I'm thirsty and by faith I drink of You, Holy Spirit, right now in Jesus' name. I now thank you, Lord, that you have filled me with the Holy Spirit. I am really truly full of the Spirit of God. Thank you so much!"

For Personal Reflection/Group Discussion:

1. Have you confessed and renounced any sin(s) that the Holy Spirit has revealed to you? This is critical in order to live a genuine, holy life. (Remember the questions in Chapter 4?)

2. Have you accepted/embraced as true what you have been learning, that is, that you have been separated from the Law and from sin as master? How do you know that this is not only biblical but that it is also true in your life?

3. As a person 'alive from the dead' (Rom.6:13,19; 12:1), have you surrendered yourself fully to Christ—as well as your past, present and future? Did He accept your full surrender?

4. Has Jesus filled you with the Holy Spirit (Eph.5:18)? How do you know?

REFERENCE NOTES TO CHAPTER FIVE

[1] Gal.5:1, 16, 24-25.

[2] Susan Maycinik, "Obedience or Performance?," *Discipleship Journal,* March/Apr 1996, 8 As written in Larson, Craig Brian, editor, *Contemporary Illustrations for Preachers, Teachers, & Writers,* Grand Rapids: Baker Books, 1996.

[3] Gal.5:2, 5, 18; Rom.6:15; Gal.5:13-14; Gal.5:5-6.

[4] Leith Anderson, "The Trouble with Legalism," *Moody* (October 1994), 15. As written in Larson, Craig Brian, editor, *Contemporary Illustrations for Preachers, Teachers, & Writers,* Grand Rapids: Baker Books, 1996, pg.135.

[5] A pamphlet entitled, *Victory through the Spirit, Gal.5:22.*

[6] Rom.1:29ff.

[7] Lk.2:40; II Cor.7:4; Gal.5:22-23.

[8] Rom.8:9.

Chapter 6

But Now:
A Life to Be Lived

By now, I hope you have experienced a clearer understanding regarding your identification with Christ. Before, you may have been trying to free yourself from sin as master. Now you know that because of Calvary, you have already been made free. Perhaps you found yourself living under the law, but now you see that you can live under God's grace with the fullness of the Spirit in your life. The Christian who has truly embraced these Scriptural truths and has received the fullness of the Spirit is a different person.

Remember Frank in Chapter 2 who was a born-again believer? He had always seen God as a judge and ruler. Then one Sunday as the minister was speaking about sonship (from Paul's Epistle to the Galatians), Frank suddenly realized that he was no longer a slave and under the 'hammer of God.' He clearly saw himself as a child, and understood that God was his heavenly Father. It was transforming. He became a different person based on that truth that he had not previously known. His prayer life and general outlook changed. Yes, Frank became a child of God at conversion years before, but this 'sonship' only became a reality in his life when he embraced that truth and lived by it.

Yet for Frank, for you, and for me there is still a life to be lived. There are the mundane, daily duties of life to perform, not to mention the trials and temptations that we face. So what do we do? Does counting on the fact of our identification with Christ and being filled with the Spirit really make a difference? Does it make a difference, for example, in how we should deal with temptation?

Temptation

Before answering that question, let's see what James teaches in his Epistle regarding temptation:

> "No one, when tempted, should say, 'I am being tempted by God'; for God cannot be tempted by evil and he himself tempts no one. But one is tempted by one's own desire, being lured and enticed by it; then, when that desire has conceived, it gives birth to sin, and that sin, when it is fully grown, gives birth to death" (Ja.1:13-15).

God never tempts us to do wrong. We are tempted when our own desires are lured, drawn out and enticed by the 'bait.' Jesus personally suffered being tempted.[1]

He desired to eat food when He was hungry, and He desired to have all the kingdoms of the world—but never out of God's timing or outside of His will. We all have strong natural desires: desires to be successful in life and work, to be accepted by others; the desire for food, sleep, sex, and comfort—to name just a few. There is nothing wrong with these desires in themselves. In fact, God created us to have these. But, when we choose to satisfy a desire in the wrong way, then, James says, we sin. For example, since we live in a world with other human beings, it's impossible for a man to not look at a woman. Yet whenever that same man chooses to look at her with an impure intent he has already committed a sin.[2]

After certain merchants brought Joseph down to Egypt, he was made overseer in the house of his master; and the Lord blessed the Egyptian's house for Joseph's sake. After a time, his master's wife began looking on him with desire and wanted him to sleep with her. He repeatedly refused to listen and kept out of her way as much as possible, but she persisted with her words day after day. Once, when no one else was in the house, she pulled at his coat and asked him to come to bed with her. Joseph slipped out of his coat and ran out of the house.[3]

There isn't any temptation that comes our way that isn't common to all of us. God can be depended upon. He won't fail us or let us be tempted beyond what we can stand. He will always see to it that in any temptation, we have a way of escape so that we can come through it victoriously. In craving to be rich, or in temptations that can lead to sexual misconduct or to idolatry or that involve other youthful passions, the "way of escape" is to stay clear of them by fleeing. That's right, in these cases the 'way out' is to avoid the temptations by running from them.[4]

Sue and Johannes had been dating for quite some time and became involved sexually, after which they decided to end their relationship. Three months later Johannes called and suggested that they go out for dinner. After some discussion and persuasion, they met at a nice restaurant. Following dinner, Johannes suggested that they take a drive around the lake. That wasn't a good idea, but after they discussed it Sue thought, "What harm is there in driving around the lake?" The full moon reflecting on the picturesque lake was a sight to be seen. Johannes thought it was a good idea for them to get out of the car to see this breathtaking sight. Sue wasn't so sure. But, "what's wrong with looking at the moon's reflection on the lake?" It didn't take long until they had sexual relations. Why? What went wrong? We need to run from sexual temptations.

Though we must flee from such temptations, we must "flee to," or "run after" a holy life. The apostle Paul says that we must pursue integrity, godliness, faith, love, peace, steadfastness, and gentleness. These are the qualities to aim at and constantly strive for. Run from the determination to be rich and from the love of money, and run after godliness; and this godliness, Paul says, must be accompanied by being content with the material provisions we have. After all, we didn't bring anything into this world and we certainly can't take anything with us when we die. Those who have a desire for wealth and keep planning to get rich open themselves up to temptations and can fall into all sorts of senseless and hurtful desires.[5]

At the same time, be aware that God's "way of escape" is not always by "fleeing." We are to be on our guard against spiritual dangers, and stand firm in our faith. As Christians, we need to be courageous and grow in strength. In Galatia, false "Christians" had been smuggled into a meeting to spy on the liberty that a group professed to have in Christ. These pseudo-Christians attempted to bind up the others with rules and regulations. But Paul said, "We did not for a moment yield to their claims" (Gal.2:4-5). We are to stand fast and keep a tight grip on the teachings of Scripture. Paul wrote to the Galatian church: "For freedom Christ has set us free. Stand firm, therefore, and do not submit to a yoke of slavery" (Gal.5:1, NRSV).[6]

When the devil tempted Jesus to turn stones into loaves of bread, He stood firm and responded with Scripture. When the tempter suggested that He throw Himself down from the highest point of the Temple since God's angels would protect Him, Jesus stood firm and responded with Scripture. When Satan promised the Lord all the kingdoms of the world and their splendor if He would only kneel down and worship him, Jesus stood His ground and answered with Scripture. Then Jesus said, "Be gone, Satan!" and the devil left Him.[7]

Like many sheep ranchers in the West, Lexy Lowler had tried about everything to stop crafty coyotes from killing her sheep. She used odor sprays, electric fences, and "scare-coyotes." She slept among the flock during the summer and placed battery-operated radios near them. She corralled them at night, and herded them by day. Yet this rancher from Montana had lost scores of lambs.

Then she discovered the llama—the aggressive, funny-looking llama. "Llamas don't appear to be afraid of anything," she said. "When they see something, they put their head up and walk straight toward it. This is aggressive behavior as far as the coyote is concerned, and they won't have anything to do with that... Coyotes are opportunists, and llamas take that opportunity away." Like llamas, we must stand up to the enemy.[8]

James says, "Submit yourselves therefore to God. Resist the devil, and he will flee from you." (Ja.4:7). Notice, we are to flee from certain temptations, but we are not to flee from the devil! We are to stand firm and be resistant. "Wear all the weapons in God's armory," Paul says. Then we can stand our ground against the cunning schemes of the devil.[9]

For Personal Reflection/Group Discussion:

1. How would James or the apostle Paul define 'temptation'?

2. What was the Apostle Paul's intent and meaning when he wrote I Cor.10:13?

3. Discuss various kinds of temptations and the 'way of escape' that God has provided for each, or think of temptations you have faced and the 'ways of escape' you have experienced.

REFERENCE NOTES TO CHAPTER FIVE

[1] Heb.2:18.
[2] Mt.5:28.
[3] Gen.39:1-12.
[4] I Cor.10:13; I Tim.1:9-11; I Cor.6:18; 10:14; II Tim.2:22.
[5] I Tim.6:1; II Tim.2:22; I Tim.6:6-9.
[6] I Cor.16:13; cf. II Thes.2:15.
[7] Mt.4:3-11.
[8] *Denver Post* as cited in *Illustrations for Preaching & Teaching from Leadership Journal;* Editor Craig Brian Larson, 1993, pg. 259 by Christianity Today, Inc.
[9] Eph.6:11-17.

Chapter 7

Sometimes We Need to Take Off Old Clothes and Put On New Ones

I had been experiencing the reality of being "dead to sin," "dead to the law," "alive unto God" and being daily "filled with the Spirit." But a note I received from a visiting friend shook my world. As I sat back in my office chair and read the note, part of it said, "You have a problem with anger." I quickly sat upright, reflected, and said to the Lord, and myself, "No I don't." I really didn't think that I had a problem with anger. But I asked the Lord to reveal the truth to me; if I had anger in my life, I wanted to know. I received no "revelation." About an hour later, I had to go home for something. My two girls were playing in the front yard doing something that I had told them about a million times (OK, I'm exaggerating) not to do. I sure got angry! Right then and there, I could plainly see that I did have a problem with anger.

I was devastated. Not only for discovering such a sin in my life that I seemed to be unaware of, but also because I was walking with the Lord and always trying to stay open to His Word. I knew that I wasn't immune to such a sin (I had a problem in the past with anger), but what was I going to do now? Ps.37:8 says to "cease from anger, and forsake wrath." I definitely wanted to refrain from anger and abandon it. Certainly I confessed it and forsook it, but it would probably come back as it was obviously a habit in my life. It was time to take off the old clothes.

You have learned (or been reminded) with regard to your former way of living that you have put off your old unregenerate self that followed the desires which can deceive you. Even so, there are times when you may discover that you need to finish with a particular sin by putting it away, or taking it off as if it were old clothing. Paul in Col.3:8 says, "But now you also, put them all aside: anger, wrath, malice, slander and abusive speech from your mouth." And that's what I needed to do, in obedience to God's Word and by faith, to put away this anger. I had already put off the old self and its habits when I had entered into the reality of Romans 6. But now I needed to rid myself of this anger that had crept in and had stayed too long. This was not the time to try to use my strong will to try to quit such a sin. Rather I needed to obey the Word and "put the anger aside"—put if off and trust the Spirit of grace to honor that obedience and make it a reality in my life.[1]

Having done this the question is now: "If I have confessed and forsaken the sin of anger and through faith have put it off, do I now believe that anger has been cleansed from my heart and that it has actually been put out of my life?"

> "Create in me a clean heart, O God, and renew a steadfast spirit within me" (Ps.51:10).

The apostle John tells us that if we confess our sins—if I freely admit that I have sinned—God can be depended upon, since He is just, to forgive us our sins, AND to purify us from all unrighteousness—that is, He will also cleanse me from all wickedness.[2] Did I believe that God would honor His Word? That He forgave me AND cleansed me from the sin of anger AND that I was rid of that sin that I had put aside by faith in His Word and in Holy Spirit? Yes I did. "If we walk in the light as he is in the light, we have fellowship with one another, and the blood of Jesus Christ his Son cleanseth us from all sin" (I Jn.1:7, KJV).

Is that it? Cleansed and no more problem? No. Notice that Paul says in Ephesians that we should not only "put off" or "put aside" sins, but we must also "put on" something. For example, if I had needed to put off lying, then I would put on the truth. Paul in Eph.4:31-32 says, "Let all bitterness and wrath and anger be put away from you, along with all malice. Be kind to one another, tenderhearted, forgiving each other just as God in Christ also has forgiven you." The apostle not only tells us to "put them all aside" but he also tells the Colossian church to "put on a heart of compassion, kindness, humility, gentleness and patience." So in the case of anger, what did I need to put on? God had told Cain, "...sin is crouching at the door; and its desire is for you, but you must master it" (Gen.4:7b). But Cain rose up against his brother Abel and killed him. I needed to put on self-control, which was exactly what I didn't have. So what was I going to do? Prov.19:11 says, "A man's discretion makes him slow to anger...". So I figured I also needed discretion. But what about the self-control? That was my problem—I had a lack of self-restraint in this area. However, the fruit of the Spirit is self-control. Once again, in obedience to the Word, I put on what was needed, that is, discretion and self-control. I trusted the Holy Spirit to make it real in my life.[3]

So you do all this and you "automatically" become "fixed" with no more problem in that area—right? Wrong. We are talking about applying God's principles in our lives, and not living by some kind of legalistic rules or computerized results at the push of a button. The Holy Spirit is a Person and desires a relationship with us. We apply the principles of the Word of God into our lives in obedience to His Word and trust the Holy Spirit to make them real in us.[4]

Whenever I fell back into anger after this, I confessed my weakness and my sin. The desire to do what was right was certainly there, but I couldn't make myself do the right thing. My own will was against my anger and I never intended to become angry, but I lacked the power to act with discretion and self-control. The solution? To receive forgiveness and complete cleansing (again), to get rid of those clothes and put on the new ones (again) and trust the Holy Spirit (again) since it is "God Himself whose power creates within you both the desire and the <u>power</u> to execute His gracious will" (Phil.2:13, Williams). It didn't take long until anger was no longer the "frequent visitor."

So what about you? Is it time to take off the old clothing and put on the new? Perhaps purity for impurity, or speaking the truth for lying, longsuffering for impatience, working for stealing, edifying speech for that which is unwholesome and corrupt, or whatever the Holy Spirit may show you. Confess it and receive cleansing, put off and put on, and trust the Lord to work out His grace in you.

For Personal Reflection/Group Discussion

1. Explain in practical terms the principle of taking off and putting on.

2. How would you explain (or draw) this principle to someone in terms of a specific sin.

3. Is there any area in your life that needs to be put off (and new clothing be put on)? If you want, you can use the following list to review your life before the Lord:

pride or independence	harshness	joy in speaking of the faults in others
love of human praise	a critical spirit	evading or covering up the truth
anger	fear of man	a disposition to worry and fret
impatience	jealousy	lack of concern for the lost
resentment	envy	selfishness
stubbornness	unbelief	indifference
unteachableness	love of money	leaving a better impression of yourself
ingratitude	unforgiveness	than is strictly true

REFERENCE NOTES TO CHAPTER SEVEN

[1] Cf. Eph.4:22, 25a; cf. Col.3:8-9.
[2] I Jn.1:9.
[3] Cf. Eph.4:25; Col.3:8, 12; Gal.5:23.
[4] II Cor.13:13

Chapter 8

Spiritual Salmon

It's dark, perverse, and has its own wisdom, pleasures, ways and worries. It gives false security. It has its own god and the majority of people live under its control. What is it?

It's the world from God's viewpoint. Not human society in general, but rather human society as a system warped by its many cares, possessions and philosophies that are hostile toward God. The world has its rudimentary notions and principles and material ways of looking at things, and they can influence our way of thinking.[1]

This is extremely important to know and understand since to be friends with the world means to be at enmity with God. In other words, whoever is bent on being friendly with the world makes himself an enemy of God. Before we were Christians we were all learning the elements of the world's knowledge. We were following the ways of the world that offer vain grandeur and glamour and provide the things our physical nature and eyes craved. Because of the new birth, we have escaped the corruption, moral decay and polluting influence, which is in the world due to lust and greed. Yet, we need to be on our guard. We can be carried away by the world's philosophies, intellectualism, or high-sounding nonsense. These are the hollow shams that people follow instead of being guided by what Christ has said.[2]

Chuck Swindoll wrote about Lana. Although the names, dates, and places had been changed, the story's theme remained the same: "one of his parishioners, Phil, had caused another Christian to stumble. This time the casualty was Lana, a nineteen-year-old whom Phil had dated for the past seven months.

"According to her parents, Phil had wooed Lana to her first taste of beer and wine, her first drug high, her first X-rated movie, and her first all-night date. I suppose you could say that his natural charm and live-and-let-live spirit attracted her like a moth to a flame. And though she struggled with his flippant attitude toward their church's moral teachings, she was captivated by his interpretation of Christian liberty. As he was fond of saying, 'Jesus set us free so we could explore life to its fullest, not so we could be held back by someone's list of do's and don'ts.' Persuaded by Phil, Lana spread her moral wings and flew into taboo airspace. There she joined a new flock of friends, saw new landscapes, and experienced new thrills. It all seemed so right, so liberating—at least for awhile.

"After five months the pleasures became oppressive demands; the scenery turned ugly and treacherous; and once-inviting, eagle-like friends showed themselves to be disgusting vultures. Lana felt the current of her lifestyle pulling her down to the point of no return, but regardless of how hard she fought, she couldn't stop falling. Alcoholism, drug addiction, and sexual escapades held her in a death grip. Desperate, she finally turned to the two people who had repeatedly proved their love—her mother and father. Through an unbroken stream of tears, she bared her soul, pleading for help. Her parents, in turn, went to their pastor seeking solace and counsel.

"As the minister listened to Lana's parents, he recalled so many confrontations with Phil. Each time he had explained to Phil that his concept of Christian freedom was unbiblical and damaging to himself and others. But each time Phil had stood his ground, refusing even to entertain the idea that he was wrong."

Yet his freedom was actually an excuse for doing wrong. This story recalls the words of Peter: "Act as free men, and do not use your freedom as a covering for evil, but use it as bondslaves of God" (I Pe.2:16), and "They promise them freedom, while they themselves are slaves of depravity--for a man is a slave to whatever has mastered him" (II Pe.2:19, NIV).

Crucified to the World and the World to You

An important principle for us to keep in mind is that "the world has been crucified to" the Christian and the Christian "has been crucified to the world" (Gal.6:14). As far as the world is concerned you are dead. The world pays attention to those who are of the world. But it separates itself from the Christian who is not part of its evil system any longer. We don't fit in. As Jesus said, "If you belonged to the world the world would love what it owned. But because you don't belong to the world and I've selected you from it, the world hates you" (Jn.15:19). Old unbelieving friends and buddies lose interest and stay away from those who serve Christ in purity.[3]

Yet the world is not only crucified to the believer, but the believer is also separated from the world. God doesn't take us out of the world, He sends us into it and will protect us from the evil one. We have died to the world's controlling system. So we as Christians must choose to separate ourselves from the world's joys, cares, appeals, pleasures, possessions and attractions. The power and victory that overcomes and defeats the world is our faith in Jesus Christ. Lana needed to learn these truths the hard way.[4]

That doesn't mean that there aren't temptations and difficulties in this world. We still have responsibilities down here on earth, and it's easy to become overly concerned with the matters of this world. Besides that, we must keep ourselves untarnished and free from its smut. This present age has it own cares, wisdom, and other futile things that seem so often to offer the best of everything, including satisfaction and fulfillment.[5] Just ask Lana. The apostle Paul tells us: "Don't let the world around you squeeze you into its own mould, but let God re-mould your minds from within, so that you may prove in practice that the plan of God for you is good, meets all His demands and moves towards the goals of true maturity" (Rom.12:2, Phillips).

Salmon are known for swimming against the current. We must be spiritual salmon who swim against the current. Lot was terribly distressed day after day by the immoral conduct of the wicked society in lawless Sodom. He swam against the current, living a righteous life there, though he saw lewd and wicked conduct. Is it any wonder we are not to fashion ourselves and imitate the humanistic ways of this present, transitory age with its superficial and external lifestyle? Instead of modeling ourselves after this age, Paul exhorts us to be transformed by the renewing of our mind, which will bring about this inward change. Then we can discern what God's will is in various areas of our life.[6]

The Renewed Mind

Our mind is so important. At the Wright Patterson Air Force base in Dayton, Ohio, researchers hope they will develop the means for pilots to fly airplanes with their minds. The project is called *brain-actuated control*.

Writers Ron Kutulak and Jon Van say that this is how it could work: the pilot would wear scalp monitors that pick up electrical signals from various points on his head. The scalp monitors would be wired to a computer. Using biofeedback techniques, the pilot would learn to manipulate the electrical activity created by his or her thought processes. The computer would translate the electrical signals into mechanical commands for the airplane.

Imagine being able to bank an airplane's wings, accelerate, and climb another ten thousand feet, all by controlling what you think.

Although controlling airplanes with the mind is yet to be developed, our mind already has tremendous control: our behavior.[7] The mind plays an extremely important role in our spiritual life. We must use our minds in order to know the Lord and to love Him. There is a great difference between a mind that is distorted, polluted, unspiritual, blinded by the god of the times and is destitute of the truth, and a mind that is renewed. A renewed mind is one that is pure and honest, understands God's Word, is spiritually sound, is under Christ's authority, and is occupied with what is above and not with the passing things of the world.[8]

Even though God illuminates our mind, prints His laws on it and is able to give us a wise and wholesome one, we still have a role to play in the renewing process. Paul in Philippians tells us what we should be thinking about: Whatever things are true, honest and dignified, just, pure, lovely and endearing; we also need to think about the fine, good things in others; our thoughts should dwell on whatever has virtue as well as anything that is praiseworthy. This means that we need to stay alert since there are many situations in the course of the day that can lead us down the wrong path of thinking. For example, at times it may be almost too easy to fall into speaking harmful words or gossip or use foolish words that don't edify. We must choose to set our minds on the 'things of the Spirit' and on God's viewpoint.[9]

Meditation

Choosing what we are going to think about is obviously very important to having new ideals and attitudes. But without a doubt the most effective way to continue to renew our mind is to meditate on the Word of God. After the death of Moses the Lord told Joshua that in order to be successful and prosperous in his dealings he was to meditate day and night on the Word of God in order to comply with everything that was in it. "How blessed is the man who does not walk in the counsel of the wicked, nor stand in the path of sinners, nor sit in the seat of scoffers! But his delight is in the law of the Lord, and in His law *he meditates* (emphasis added) day and night. He will be like a tree firmly planted by streams of water, which yields its fruit in its season and its leaf does not wither; and in whatever he does, he prospers" (Ps.1:1-3). A fruitful life belongs to those who meditate on the Word of God and obey it. The Psalmist treasured God's Word in his heart so that he would not sin against the Lord. Do you want to have more understanding, discernment and a better grasp of the truth? You will, if you meditate on the Word of God![10]

What is meditation? Some may think that meditation is just sitting still, keeping one's mind thoughtless and empty, and trusting that God will fill it with His words. However, Biblical meditation involves fixing one's mind on the Word of God, actively reflecting upon it and pondering it as we trust the Holy Spirit for help in understanding and applying the Word. Consider the following:

- First, even before we open our Bibles we should sincerely ask the Lord for wisdom and the knowledge of Himself. Ask the Holy Spirit to teach you in His Word (cf. Prov.2:3-6; Jn.15:26) and to enlighten your mind to understand it (cf. Lk.24:45).

- As we open the Scriptures to a particular text, we must then seek to discover what the author meant when the passage was written. The question to ask, therefore, is not "What do I think the text means to me?" or "How do I feel about it?" but rather, "What did God want the original hearers/audience to understand?"

- Then, as we reflect on the Word, we must take to heart what the Lord has said. That is, there needs to be a personal acceptance and receiving of the written Word for ourselves (cf. Prov.2:1-2).

- Finally, we must ask: How do we apply and obey the Bible text that we have just meditated upon?

The Will of God

The reason for or result of letting ourselves be transformed by renewal of the mind is so that we may discern what the will of God is. Paul teaches us in Rom.12:2 that in order to know if something is God's will, it must first be tested.

Some years ago, a speedboat driver who had survived a racing accident described what had happened. He said that he had been at near top speed when his boat veered slightly and hit a wave at a dangerous angle. The combined force of his speed and the size and angle of the wave sent the boat spinning crazily into the air. He was thrown from his seat and propelled deeply into the water—so deep, in fact, that he had no idea which direction the surface was. He had to remain calm and wait for the buoyancy of his life vest to begin pulling him up. Once he discovered which way was up, he could swim for the surface.

Sometimes we find ourselves surrounded by confusing options, too deeply immersed in our problems to know "which way is up." When this happens, we too should remain calm, waiting for God's gentle tug to pull us in the proper direction.[11] So what is our "life vest" that pulls us in the right direction? The Word of God, the Holy Spirit, and circumstances are three.

Bob Mumford, in *Take Another Look at Guidance*, compares discovering God's will with a sea captain's docking procedure:[12]

> A certain harbor in Italy can be reached only by sailing up a narrow channel between dangerous rocks and shoals. Over the years, many ships have been wrecked because navigation is hazardous.

> To guide the ships safely into port, three lights have been mounted on three huge poles in the harbor. When the three lights are perfectly lined up and seen as one, the ship can safely proceed up the narrow channel. If the pilot sees two or three lights, he knows he's off course and in danger.

God has provided three beacons to guide us. The same rules of navigation apply—the three lights must be lined up before it is safe for us to proceed. These three harbor lights of guidance are again:

1. The Word of God: this leads us and confirms our guidance when the direction is fully consistent and in agreement with the principles and teachings of Scripture.

2. The Holy Spirit: He gives clarity, conviction and peace in our hearts. "Yes, this is the way I should go." One's mind and heart are kept in perfect peace that is deeper than our knowledge and surpasses our understanding.

3. Circumstances: those "coincidences" in life that confirm God's leading, as well as the counsel and approval of mature and wise believers.

If what we believe to be God's will passes all three "tests" we can rest assured that it is God's direction for us. If any one of these tests is "out of line," then we wait for God to clarify His will. God's will is good and beneficial, pleasing and without error.

To not mix or associate with those who belong to the world certainly doesn't mean that we are not to have any contact at all with those outside the church. God does not want us to isolate ourselves from human society! But we need to be continually renewed in our minds so that we can live as light and salt in this world, dark and needy as it is.[13]

For Personal Reflection/Group Discussion

1. What is the "world"? How can you be a "spiritual salmon" in the world? Explain Gal.6:14.

2. What is a "renewed mind"? What does it have to do with a Christian living in this world?

3. Meditate on John 15 or a passage of your choice. What did you learn and how did you apply it?

4. How would you use the "harbor lights" of guidance in a practical way?

REFERENCE NOTES TO CHAPTER EIGHT

[1] Col.2:20a.

[2] Ja.4:4; cf. Gal.4:3; cf. Eph.2:2; I Jn.2:16; II Pe.1:4;2:20; Col.2:8.

[3] Cf. I Jn.4:5.

[4] Cf. Jn.17:15,18; I Jn.5:4-5.

[5] Cf. I Cor.7:33-34; Ja.1:27; cf. Mt.13:22; I Cor.1:20.

[6] II Pe.2:7-8; Rom.12:2.

[7] Larson, Craig Brian, Ed., *Contemporary Illustrations for Preachers, Teachers & Writers*, Baker Books: Grand Rapids: MI, 1996; pg. 153.

[8] I Jn.5:20; Mt.22:37; II Pe.3:1; Lk.24:45; I Pe.4:7; II Tim. 1:7; Col.3:2.

[9] Lk.24:45; Heb.8:10; Eph.1:8; II Tim.1:7; Phil.4:8; Rom.8:6

[10] Josh.1:8; Ps.119:9,11, 99-100.

[11] Larson, Craig Brian, *Illustrations for Preaching & Teaching from Leadership Journal*, Christianity Today, Inc & Baker Book House Co., 1993, pg.174.

[12] *Ibid*, pg.108.

[13] Cf. I Cor.5:5-10.

Chapter 9

Jimminy Cricket

Mr. Cherry, a carpenter, found a piece of wood that wept and laughed like a child. He gave the piece of wood to his friend, Geppetto, who takes it to make himself a marionette that will dance, fence and turn somersaults. As soon as he gets home, Geppetto fashions the marionette and calls it—you guessed it—Pinocchio.[1]

Later Pinocchio has a small friend, Jimminy Cricket, who tries his best to keep Pinocchio out of trouble. Unfortunately Pinocchio doesn't listen to that small voice and keeps getting into trouble. We all have a Jimminy Cricket, but it goes by another name... our conscience, which distinguishes right from wrong.

Since one day both the righteous and the unrighteous will be judged, Paul writes that he does his best to always maintain "a blameless conscience both before God and before men" (Acts 24:16). The apostle lived his life in the presence of God with a clear conscience.[2]

According to *Time* magazine, in 1970 Katherine Power, a student at Brandeis University in Boston, was a leader of the radical National Student Strike Force. She and several others planned to raise money to buy arms for the Black Panthers by robbing a bank.

Kathy drove the getaway car. But the robbery went awry. Patrolman Walter Schroeder quickly answered a silent alarm. Shots were fired by one of Kathy's accomplices, and patrolman Schroeder was killed.

That night Kathy began what would be twenty-three years of life on the run. Listed as armed and "very dangerous", she was on the FBI's most-wanted list.

In the late 1970's, Power moved to Oregon. There she assumed the name Alice Metzinger, settled down, started a new life in the restaurant business, bought a house, gave birth to her son, and married. She was an active part of the community and seemingly had every reason to be at peace.

But at age forty-four Kathy Power was desperately tired, tormented by guilt, and chronically depressed. Finally Kathy did the only thing she felt she could to end her agony. In Sept. 1993, she turned herself in to the Boston police.[3] Her conscience was doing its job.

Paul in his letter to Timothy urged his own "son in the faith" to remain in Ephesus. Paul was going on to Macedonia. He wanted Timothy to caution certain persons not to invent new doctrines and busy themselves with legends and never-ending genealogies. These things, he said, only stir up questions and arguments rather than further God's divine plan.[4] But the goal of his instruction was love, which comes "from a pure heart and a good conscience and sincere faith" (I Tim.1:5).

In *Focus on the Family*, Rolf Zettersten writes:

"A good friend in North Carolina bought a new car with a voice-warning system... At first Edwin was amused to hear the soft female voice gently remind him that his seat belt wasn't fastened... Edwin affectionately called this voice the 'little woman.'

"He soon discovered his little woman was programmed to warn him about his gasoline. 'Your fuel level is low,' she said one time in her sweet voice. Edwin nodded his head and thanked her. He figured he still had enough to go another fifty miles, so he kept on driving. But a few minutes later, her voice interrupted again with the same warning. And so it went over and over. Although he knew it was the same recording, Edwin thought her voice sounded harsher each time.

"Finally, he stopped his car and crawled under the dashboard. After a quick search, he found the appropriate wires and gave them a good yank. So much for the 'little woman.'

"He was still smiling to himself a few miles later when his car began sputtering and coughing. He ran out of gas! Somewhere inside the dashboard, Edwin was sure he could hear the little woman laughing."[5] Ignoring the little voice can be costly.

Paul instructed Timothy to cling tightly to his faith in Christ and to always keep his conscience clear. It was through spurning their consciences that certain persons had wrecked their lives regarding the faith.[6]

Is it any wonder that Peter exhorts us to give honor to Christ in our hearts as Lord, to always be ready to give (in a gentle and respectful way) an answer to anyone who asks us a reason for the hope that we cherish, and to keep our conscience clear with good Christian conduct?[7]

It's obvious from the Scriptures that a clear conscience is vital. Yet it is also important to understand that knowledge influences one's conscience. Having been missionaries in Brazil, my wife and I know that in certain parts of the country, eating meat that has been sacrificed to idols is a troubling matter for some Christians. It's true that an idol-god has no real existence in this world. An idol isn't really a god since there is only one God. However, people have assumed that there are so-called "gods" in the sky and down here on earth—gods and lords galore, in fact. There is only one God and one Lord. Yet all Christians don't have such knowledge. There are those who have been accustomed to idols and still regard certain meat as food sacrificed to a god. With their conscience being weak on this issue, they incur guilt and their conscience is polluted if they eat. Knowledge influences our conscience.[8]

José knows that God's approval or acceptance of him is not a matter of meat and it isn't based on the food he eats. He is quite aware that he has no advantage with God by eating meat, and he is not going to fall short by abstaining. So José has no problem partaking of food that's been offered in sacrifice. However, he encourages his Christian friend, Miguel, to eat the food that has been offered to an idol, and Miguel has a weak conscience. What could happen? Would José be fortifying Miguel's conscience by getting him to eat such food? Absolutely not. He will actually be causing Miguel to violate the misgivings of his doubtful conscience by eating such food. José will cause his brother to sin, he will wound Miguel's weak conscience, and ultimately José will sin against Christ Himself. José's freedom to eat such meat can become a stumbling block to Miguel. So, if eating meat makes your brother sin, never eat such meat again rather than be the occasion of your brother or sister's sin. This is what love is all about.[9]

Jeff and Robert were active Christians in their church and were very good friends. Jeff was over scrupulous in his faith regarding drinking and not eating meat on Fridays. Robert's faith, on the other hand, allowed him to drink, and he had no problem eating meat on Friday. God accepts both of these believers. Yet as time passed, Robert began to look down on Jeff, and Jeff began to judge Robert. Issues such as these can cause major problems between Christians. In this case, it reached the point that the only reason Robert welcomed Jeff into his house was to dispute their opinions.[10]

In reality, there isn't anything intrinsically "unholy" in food or drink. But, whatever a person thinks is unclean is unclean to him or her. And, any action that does not stem from faith and rest on conviction is sin. God wants each one to be fully convinced in his own mind what he should do in regards to non-essential matters such as what and when to eat and drink.[11]

Robert was providing an occasion for Jeff to fall. Jeff was seriously upset because Robert was eating and drinking and trying to get him to do the same. Jeff's conscience was becoming tripped up or entangled; he could stumble and fall. Where was Christian love? How was Robert being governed by love when his eating and persuading could induce Jeff to sin? "Love does no harm to its neighbor" (Rom.13:10a, NIV). Robert should have been a support, bearing with Jeff's weakness. He should have been trying to "please his neighbor" to help him grow.[12]

Robert needed to responsibly exercise the freedom he had in Christ. It was important for both of them to remember the ways of the Kingdom: God's kingdom doesn't consist of eating and drinking; but of rightness of heart, peace, and joy though the presence of the Holy Spirit. This is what is acceptable to God and wins the approval of people. Both Robert and Jeff needed to begin pursuing the things that would contribute to peace and to building one another up. Everything is permissible for Christians but not everything is beneficial. All things are lawful but not everything builds up our character.[13]

Blessed is the Christian whose practices in non-essential matters don't go beyond her own conscience. Blessed is the one who has no qualms or misgivings about what he allows himself to do. And at the same time, blessed is the Christian man or woman who is not always looking after his own welfare, but rather seeks the good of others.[14]

Paul wrote, "I thank God whom I worship, as did my forefathers, with a pure conscience" (II Tim.1:3a, KNOX).

For Personal Reflection/Group Discussion:

1. Cheryl and Rita are having trouble over the matter of

jewelry and clothing. Cheryl condemns Rita for some of the things she wears. Yet Rita tells her that if she were going out with Jesus, she would wear those things. How would you counsel these two in light of this chapter?

2. What do you believe regarding matters such as movies, tattoos, body piercing, types of music, and dancing? How did you arrive at your conclusions? How has your background, culture or knowledge influenced your convictions?

3. Read I Corinthians10:23-33. Why should a Christian's personal freedom be limited by another's conscience?

4. Musa's conscience began to convince him that he should be washing his hands more carefully and diligently before eating. It got to the point that Musa knew that it was becoming excessive and unnecessary, yet his conscience bothered him. How could Musa "correct" his conscience by applying God's Word in Matthew 15:1-2,11; Mark 7:1-6,15?

REFERENCE NOTES TO CHAPTER NINE

[1] *Adventures of Pinocchio,* by Carlo Collodi, ClassicReader.com.
[2] Cf. Acts 23:1.
[3] Larson, Brian Craig, *Contemporary Illustrations for Preachers, Teachers, & Writers.* Grand Rapids: MI. Baker Books. 1996, pg.98.
[4] I Tim.1:3-4.
[5] Larson, Brian Craig, Editor. *Illustrations for Preaching & Teaching from Leadership Journal.* Christianity Today and Baker Book House, 1993, pg.39.
[6] I Tim.1:19.
[7] I Pe.3:15-16.
[8] Cf. I Cor.8:4-7.
[9] I Cor.8:8; cf. I Cor.8:9-13.
[10] Cf. Rom.14:1-4.
[11] Rom.14:14, 23.
[12] Rom.15:1-2.
[13] Cf. Rom. 14:13, 15, 17-19.
[14] I Cor. 10:24,33.

Chapter 10

Abiding

What does the phrase "in Christ" mean to you personally? This is an extremely important question. For example, it means that "in Christ" we have eternal life. There is also deliverance, sanctification, freedom, justification, the blessing of Abraham, God's grace—in a word: salvation. We are a new creation—a new person altogether "in Christ."[1]

Everything that pertains to salvation and our Christian walk is related to us being "in Christ." God's grace is given to us in Christ. There is no condemnation for those who are in Him. Also, remember when the apostle urged the Romans to consider themselves as having ended their relation to sin but living in unbroken relation to God? "Count yourselves dead to sin but alive to God in Christ Jesus" (Rom.6:11, NIV). In fact, through our union with Him, the Holy Spirit, who gives us life, has set us free from sin and death.[2]

And not only are we in Christ, He is also "in us". We can say with the apostle Paul, "Christ lives in me" (Gal.2:20). The two principles, Christ in us and we in Him, are key to the victorious Christian life.

When Jesus was praying to His heavenly Father in John 17, He not only interceded for His disciples, but for us as well. He prayed that we all might be one. Just as the Father lived in Him and He in the Father, Jesus requested that we also would be in union with them so that the world would be convinced that the Father had sent the Son. Perfectly united, we would be made completely one. This not only has great implications in our relationship to other Christians, but it is extremely important to understand our "abiding" relationship with Christ.[3]

Please bear with me. In John 15, Jesus pictured Himself as the true Vine and His Father as the Gardener or Vinedresser. Any barren branch in Him—any that doesn't bear fruit—the Father cuts off; and any branch that does bear fruit He prunes so that it will bear more fruit.[4]

Then, He tells His disciples to abide in Him—that is, to remain united to Him—and He will abide in them. Here is an important teaching to understand: As a branch cannot bear fruit unless it continues to share the life of the vine, so neither can we bear fruit unless we abide in Christ. Jesus is the Vine and we are the branches. Whoever remains in union with Him—abides in Him—and He in union with them, will bear abundant fruit. Why? Because without Him, we cannot do anything of eternal value. We are like the tree that is purposely planted by running water which will produce fruit in its expected season; our leaves will never wither. So success will attend all that we do.[5]

Haroldo was a great singer, and could he preach! People were blessed because of his gifts, and fruit was evident in his life. But Haroldo had one problem. He didn't understand the importance of his abiding relationship with Christ. As time went on, even though Haroldo's singing and preaching improved, the results did not. He couldn't understand it.

Along the way, Haroldo had begun to trust more in his talents than he did in Christ's life and enablement. In order to reach others with the gospel more effectively, he turned to philosophy to understand his audience better. Also, with trust in the strengths that God had given him, he approached people and tried to sway them with subtle arguments, clever talk and the persuasive language of philosophy that he was learning.

One day as he was preparing a message he came across John 15. The words, "apart from Me you can do nothing" (v.5b), stood out to him. As he thought and prayed about those words, he began to see that his faith was resting on his own cleverness. No more. He saw that the words he would sing and the gospel he would proclaim needed the convincing power of the Holy Spirit instead of the wisdom of the age.

Haroldo directed his attention back to his need to depend upon Christ for power and success in ministry instead of on clever words and the gifts and talents that God had given him. Oh, he was still going to work hard, but the difference now was that he would depend upon God's grace working with him as he sang and preached. He was in Christ and Christ was in him.

Up until this time, Haroldo had thought of himself as sufficient for any task. "I can do anything I want to do." Now, he began to realize that true competency came only through his abiding relationship with Christ. It wasn't about his talents, his intelligence and discernment, or his ability to study and organize; it was about Christ and what Christ's life would produce through this 'branch.' He needed to humble himself, renounce his own self-sufficiency, and depend wholly upon Christ's ability and life. He wanted the Apostle Paul's words to be his: "like a man of sincerity, like a man that is sent from God and living in His presence, in union with Christ I speak His message" (II Cor.2:17b, Williams). What a difference these truths made in Haroldo's life!

Is there a difference in your life? Are you living in an abiding relationship with Christ or is there a problem with the "flow" of life between the Vine and the branch? How can you know if you are truly abiding in Him? The apostle John helps us. We know we are in an abiding union with Jesus if:[6]

- We keep Christ's commandments, especially to put our trust in Him and to love others.
- The Spirit whom He has given us testifies and gives evidence of our abiding relationship with Christ.

- We do not live in sin.

- We are living as Jesus Himself lived here on earth.

- We know that we will not shrink back in shame from Christ at His coming.

If we need to admit that our life is not consistent with one who is abiding in Christ, then we must confess our specific sins and blockages to the flow of life from the Vine. We must renounce and forsake those sins, receive Christ's forgiveness and cleansing, and put our total trust in His sufficiency and life.

Notice Jesus' words in John 15:7, "If you abide in Me, and My words abide in you, ask whatever you wish, and it will be done for you." We can ask whatever we please and we shall have it! How can this be? It's dependent upon our remaining vitally united with Christ and His words continuing to live in our hearts. Listen to Jesus' stark words: "Truly, truly, I say to you, unless you eat the flesh of the Son of Man and drink His blood, you have no life in yourselves. He who eats My flesh and drinks My blood has eternal life, and I will raise him up on the last day. For My flesh is true food, and My blood is true drink. He who eats My flesh and drinks My blood abides in Me, and I in him… he who eats Me, he also will live because of Me" (Jn.6:53-57b). Believing on Christ means feeding on Him in our hearts, by faith and partaking of His life.[7] This speaks of a very intimate and real abiding in Christ.

To what point has God's word found its home in our heart? It does so by our receiving, understanding and applying it. We must learn to inwardly "digest" God's Word as we meditate on it, chew it over, and swallow it. Jesus said, "If you continue—or abide—in My word, you are truly My disciples" (Jn.5:31).[8]

As we've seen, our abiding relationship with Christ is of utmost importance. John tells us in his first epistle that we are to continue to live in union with Jesus so that when He appears, we may have confidence and not be ashamed when we meet Him at His coming. If we abide in Christ then we should be living as He lived here on earth. If we are in union with Him and He in us, then we will keep His commandments and walk in love toward others. And we can be sure that we abide in Him, and He in us because "He has given us some measure of His Spirit" (I Jn.4:13, TCNT).

For Personal Reflection/Group Discussion:

1. What does it mean to "abide in Christ"? Give an analogy (other than the vine and branch).

2. Discuss Haroldo's "problem" and how we can learn from it.

3. How are the two principles of "Christ in us" and "us in Christ" keys to the victorious Christian life?

REFERENCE NOTES TO CHAPTER TEN

[1] Rom.6:23, 3:24; I Cor.1:2; Gal.2:4, 17; 3:14; Eph.3:6; II Tim.2:1, 10; II Cor. 5:17.
[2] I Cor.1:4; Rom.8:1; cf. Rom.8:2.
[3] Jn.17:20-21, 23.
[4] Jn.15:1-2.
[5] Jn.15:45; Ps.1:3.
[6] I Jn.3:23-24, 3:6, 2:6, 28.
[7] Bullinger, E.W., *Figures of Speech Used in the Bible*. Baker Book House, 1968; originally published in 1898 by Messrs. Eyre and Spottiswoode, in London; pgs.826-827.
[8] Cf. Jn.5:38
[9] I Jn.2:6, 28; 3:24; 4:12, 16; cf. I Jn.2:10.

Chapter 11

To Suffer or Not to Suffer: Tested Faith

Tough days. We all have them. Some are worse than others. Like the one a hard-hat employee reported on his accident form:

> "When I got to the building, I found that the hurricane had knocked off some bricks around the top. So, I rigged up a beam with a pulley at the top of the building and hoisted up a couple barrels full of bricks. When I had fixed the damaged area, there were a lot of bricks left over. Then I went to the bottom and began releasing the line. Unfortunately, the barrel of bricks was much heavier than I was—and before I knew what was happening the barrel started coming down, jerking me up.

> "I decided to hang on since I was too far off the ground by then to jump, and halfway up I met the barrel of bricks coming down fast. I received a hard blow on my shoulder. I then continued to the top, banging my head against the beam and getting my fingers pinched and jammed in the pulley. When the barrel hit the ground hard, it burst its bottom, allowing the bricks to spill out.

"I was now heavier than the barrel. So I started down again at high speed. Halfway down I met the barrel coming up fast and received severe injuries to my shins. When I hit the ground, I landed on the pile of spilled bricks, getting several painful cuts and deep bruises. At this point I must have lost my presence of mind, because I let go of my grip on the line. The barrel came down fast—giving me another blow on my head and putting me in the hospital.

"I respectfully request sick leave."[1]

Ouch. That was a tough time. We've all experienced them in one form or another. Sometimes suffering involves committing a sin against ourselves and other times against another person.

There are also the times when we do what is right and yet suffer for it. The perfect example is Christ, who was insulted and treated badly many times. He never sinned nor was anything malicious or deceitful ever heard from His lips. He also suffered and died to atone for our sins "the Just for the unjust that He might bring us to God" (I Pe.3:18a).

The reason Jesus' suffering is so important to remember is that it is to this kind of life to which we have been called. Peter made it clear that Jesus suffered on our behalf, and we should follow in His footsteps. When He was reviled and insulted He made no retort, and when He suffered He didn't threaten anybody. What He did do was commit His case into the hands of the righteous Judge. That is, He turned the matter over to His heavenly Father.[2]

If we do wrong and suffer for it, what credit is there in patiently taking the deserved punishment? On the other hand, if we do right and suffer for it patiently, this does win God's approval and is acceptable to Him.[3]

One day, the chancellor of the University of Glasgow introduced to the young men of that university, "God's missionary",

David Livingstone. When Livingstone stood up and walked to the front of the platform to speak to the group of university men, the students looked at him earnestly. They saw his hair burned crisp under the torrid tropical sun. They saw his body wasted and emaciated from jungle fever. They saw his right arm hanging limp at his side, destroyed by the attack of a ferocious African lion. When the students looked at Livingstone they stood up in one accord, in awe and silence before God's missionary.[4]

After the first century Jewish Court had the Apostles flogged, they ordered them to not speak anymore of Jesus, and then they released them. Luke tells us that the Apostles left the Sanhedrin "rejoicing because they had been counted worthy of suffering disgrace for the Name" (Acts 5:41, NIV). Paul wrote to the Philippian church, "For to you it has been granted for Christ's sake, not only to believe in Him, but also to suffer for His sake" (Phil.1:29). Also to Timothy, "Everyone who wants to live a godly life in Christ Jesus will be persecuted" (II Tim.3:12, NIV). Furthermore, Peter tells his readers that even if they have to suffer for the sake of what is right, they are still blessed, and they shouldn't be afraid of people's threats, nor be troubled by them.[5]

So what should we do when experiencing such persecution or adversity? The Scriptures come to our rescue with the following principles:

1. Entrust our lives into the hands of our faithful Creator (I Pe.4:19b).

2. Do not return evil for evil (I Pe.2:23; 3:9).

3. Keep doing what is right (I Pe.4:19c), even toward our enemies (Rom12:20).

4. Leave our case in the hands of the Judge who judges righteously (I Pe.2:23; Rom.12:19).

5. Love, pray for and bless our persecutors (Mt.5:44; Lk.6:27-28).

Well, persecution is one thing, but what about the trials that occur in all of our lives? Perhaps it's in the form of close friends moving to another place, an accident, a separation or divorce, abuse, financial difficulties, a severe illness or death in the family, or other troubles and hardships. What does God have in mind when He lets His own children suffer trials and persecution?

A man found the cocoon of an emperor moth and took it home to watch it emerge. One day a small opening appeared, and for several hours the moth struggled but couldn't seem to force its body past a certain point.

Deciding something was wrong, the man took scissors and snipped the remaining bit of cocoon. The moth emerged easily, its body large and swollen, the wings small and shriveled.

He expected that in a few hours the wings would spread out in their natural beauty, but they didn't. Instead of developing into a creature free to fly, the moth spent its life dragging around a swollen body and shriveled wings.

The constricting cocoon and the struggle necessary to pass through the tiny opening are God's way of forcing fluid from the body into the wings. The "merciful" snip was, in reality, cruel. Sometimes the struggle is exactly what we need.[6]

James, in his epistle, writes: "Consider it pure joy, my brothers, whenever you face trials of many kinds" (Ja.1:2, NIV). In other words, count it nothing but joy whenever you find yourself surrounded by various trials. Why? "Because the testing of your faith develops perseverance" (Ja.1:3, NIV). That's not all: We're to let endurance finish its work so that we can be mature and perfectly equipped, not coming up short in anything.[7]

On a commuter flight from Portland, Maine to Boston, Henry Dempsey (the pilot) heard an unusual noise near the rear of the small aircraft. He turned the controls over to his co-pilot and went back to check it out.

As he reached the tail section, the plane hit an air pocket, and Dempsey was tossed against the rear door. He quickly discovered the source of the mysterious noise. The rear door hadn't been properly latched prior to takeoff, and it flew open. He was instantly sucked out of the jet.

The co-pilot, seeing the red light that indicated an open door, radioed the nearest airport, requesting permission to make an emergency landing. He reported that the pilot had fallen out of the plane, and he requested a helicopter search of that area of the ocean.

After the plane landed, they found Henry Dempsey—holding onto the outdoor ladder of the aircraft. Somehow he had caught the ladder, held on for ten minutes as the plane flew 200 mph at an altitude of 4,000 feet, and then, at landing, kept his head from hitting the runway, which was a mere twelve inches away. It took the airport personnel several minutes to pry Dempsey's fingers from the ladder.[8] Talk about endurance and perseverance!

God wants the difficulties and trials of life that come our way to serve a good purpose. He wants to see our faith mature. Peter wrote to his readers, "… for a little while you may have had to suffer grief in all kinds of trials. These have come so that your faith—of greater worth than gold, which perishes even though refined by fire—may be proved genuine and may result in praise, glory and honor when Jesus Christ is revealed" (I Pe.1:6-7, NIV). How often do we become distressed by various trials? Yet God wants them to serve a good purpose in our lives—that our tested faith be found genuine and result in praise and honor at Christ's appearing.

And this tested faith also develops and produces perseverance. We learn to "hold on" and "keep swimming round."

> Two frogs fell into a deep cream bowl,
> One was an optimistic soul;
> But the other took the gloomy view,
> "We shall drown," he cried, without more ado.

So with a last despairing cry,
He flung his legs and said, "Good-bye."
Quoth the other frog with a merry grim,
"I can't get out, but I won't give in
I'll just swim round till my strength is spent,
Then will I die the more content."
Bravely he swam till it would seem
His struggles began to churn the cream.
On top of the butter at last he stopped,
And out of the bowl he gaily hopped.
What of the moral? 'Tis easily found:
If you can't hop out, keep swimming round.[9]

Notice the difference in *attitude* between the two frogs. It made all the difference in the end results.

Speaking from his experience as a prisoner in the Nazi concentration camps, psychiatrist Dr. Viktor Frankl said, "Everything can be taken from a man but one thing: the last of the human freedoms—to choose one's attitude in any given set of circumstances, to choose one's own way."

Charles Swindoll says it this way: "Attitude is more important than the past, than education, than money, than circumstances, than what other people think or say or do. It is more important than appearance, giftedness, or skill. It will make or break a company, a church, a home.

"The remarkable thing is, we have a choice every day regarding the attitude we will embrace for that day. We cannot change our past. We cannot change the fact that people will act in certain ways. We cannot change the inevitable. The only thing we can do is play on the one string we have, and that is our attitude."[10]

We see this played out in the life of the apostle Paul. To prevent him from thinking too highly of himself (because he saw so many magnificent revelations) Paul was given a sharp pain in his body—a thorn in his flesh that came as Satan's messenger. Three times he prayed to the Lord to relieve him of it. Yet God's answer was: My grace is sufficient for you—it's all you need, for My strength finds its full scope in your weakness.[11]

Paul's attitude then changed. He writes, "Most gladly, therefore, I will rather boast about my weaknesses, so that the power of Christ may dwell in me. Therefore, I am well content with weaknesses, with insults, with distresses, with persecutions, with difficulties, for Christ's sake; for when I am weak, then I am strong" (II Cor. 9b-10). Being content with such hardships came as the result of a revelation from the Lord. Paul saw that his very weakness made him strong in Christ. That's why he could be content with such humiliating circumstances.

For the Christian, there is not just the hope of future joy. We can be full of joy here and now even in our trials and troubles. Afflictions and suffering bring about perseverance. And this endurance works in us strength of character. This tested character produces hope—a hope that never disappoints.[12]

No matter what you and I go through, we need to keep our attitude right and our trust in the One whose plan is always good for us.

For Personal Reflection/Group Discussion:

1. Discuss or write your "theology" of persecution and troubles.

2. What is your attitude when difficulties come your way? Which "frog" are you and why?

3. What are the good things that God wants to develop in your life as you pass through hardships?

REFERENCE NOTES TO CHAPTER ELEVEN

[1] Michael Green, *Illustrations for Biblical Preaching.* As told in Swindoll, Charles R., *The Tale of the Tardy Oxcart.* Nashville, Word Publishing, 1998, pgs.21-22. Used by permission of Thomas Nelson, Inc.

[2] I Pe. 2:21, 23.

[3] I Pe.2:20.

[4] W.A Criswell, *Expository Sermons on Galatians.* As told in Swindoll, Charles R., *The Tale of the Tardy Oxcart.* Nashville, Word Publishing, 1998, pg. 580. Used by permission of Thomas Nelson, Inc.

[5] I Pe.3:14; cf.Mt.5:10-12.

[6] Larson, Craig Brian, ed., *Illustrations for Preaching and Teaching from Leadership Journal,* Grand Rapids: Baker Books, 1993, pg.266.

[7] Ja.1:4.

[8] Larson, Craig Brian, ed., *Illustrations for Preaching and Teaching from Leadership Journal,* Grand Rapids: Baker Books, 1993, pg.114.

[9] Walter Knight, *Knight's Master Book of New Illustrations.* As told in Swindoll, Charles R., *The Tale of the Tardy Oxcart.* Nashville, Word Publishing, 1998, pgs. 440-441. Used by permission of Thomas Nelson, Inc.

[10] Charles Swindoll, from *Strengthening Your Grip,* as seen in *Reader's Digest,* (February 1995).

[11] II Cor.12:7-9a.

[12] Rom.5:3-5a.

Chapter 12

That Word, "Faith"

On April 28, 1996, a gunman walked into a crowded café in Port Arthur, Australia, and started shooting. Tony Kistan, a Salvation Army soldier from Sydney, and his wife Sarah were in the restaurant when the bullets began to fly. Courageously, Tony stepped in front of his wife to shield her from the gunfire, and he was one of the first to fall. Thirty-four victims eventually died in the incident, including Tony Kistan. As he lay dying in his wife's arms, he spoke his last words, "I'm going to be with the Lord".

Those final words were quoted by the Australian media and carried to the world. At a press conference, Tony's 24-year-old son Nesan, explained why his dad held this assurance and described his father's dedication to the gospel. Hardened journalists and photographers were seen wiping tears from their eyes. In life, Tony had been a man who witnessed for his Lord to strangers and friends alike, and now in death, he had witnessed to others through his simple last statement of faith.[1]

Faith, that word, "faith". Faith lies at the heart of the gospel and is vital to living the Christian life. It was by faith that we were brought into right standing with God and became His children. His wrath was removed from us, we were sanctified and our hearts were purified...through faith.[2]

We also stand by faith and we guide our lives by it. Paul says it this way: "we walk by faith, not by sight" (II Cor. 5:7). God expects us to lead our lives by faith, and not by what we see. That's what God required of the Old Testament saints as well: Faith made Abel offer God a better and more acceptable sacrifice than Cain did. Being forewarned by God concerning events of which there was no visible sign, it was faith that enabled Noah to construct the ark. Urged on by faith, Abraham set out without any idea of where he was going. And it was faith that made him go to live as an immigrant in the Promised Land. It was because of faith that the walls of Jericho fell down after they had been marched around for seven days. There are so many other examples of faith, such as in the lives of Moses, Gideon, Samson, David and the prophets.[3]

But what is faith, and how do you describe it? These are important questions since the Scripture says that without faith you can never please God. Faith believes in and trusts God. It is confident dependence upon Him and His word. Faith involves entrusting ourselves to Him in complete confidence.[4]

Faith is really the confident assurance of something we hope for. It gives substance and a reality to our hopes; they are realized through our faith. But faith is also conviction of the reality of the things we don't see. It makes us certain of such realities. Even though something isn't revealed to the senses, faith perceives it as real. Sarah was past the age of childbearing. Yet it was faith in God's promise that enabled her to conceive. Why? Because she believed that God was faithful to do what He said He would do. Barren as she was, Sarah believed that she could rely upon Him. Faith is not a "blind leap in the dark." Rather, it is based upon evidence—the solid Word of God.[5]

Notice then that Sarah believed what the Lord told her and she believed Him. Paul says that faith comes from hearing about Christ; in other words, it comes from hearing the Word. When many Corinthians listened to Paul, they became believers in Christ. The Samaritan people had been dazzled with Simon's magic for a considerable period of time. But when Phillip came and preached the good news to them, they believed him and were baptized. However the message preached doesn't profit or benefit anyone when it isn't mixed with faith.[6]

Though the above examples refer to hearing the gospel, the principle of faith blending with the Word is far reaching and of utmost importance. When a fig tree instantly withered away at Jesus' word, the disciples were astonished and asked Him how the tree had withered so suddenly. Jesus' answer is both revealing and helpful to us: "Truly I say to you, if you have faith and do not doubt, you will not only do what was done to the fig tree, but even if you say to this mountain, 'Be taken up and cast into the sea,' it will happen. And all things you ask in prayer, believing, you will receive" (Mt.21:21-22). John in his epistle says, "This is the confidence that we have before Him, that, if we ask anything according to His will, He hears us. And if we know that He hears us in whatever we ask, we know that we have the requests which we have asked from Him" (I Jn.5:14-15). Whenever we approach God and ask Him anything that is in accordance with His will, we can rest assured that He will give us what we have asked for. So, whatever we ask in prayer, we will receive, if we have faith and if our request is according to God's will.[7]

Ted and Mary had saved as much money as they could for their daughter's college. She was now ready to leave for school but the necessary funds were not there. The couple knew that God wanted them to trust Him for the finances but they had never had to 'trust' Him for so much money. Ted tried to believe as he prayed but his confidence always gave way to doubt. He felt like the billowing sea where they spent their previous vacation—being driven and blown about by the wind. He was also feeling like a man with two minds, wavering at every turn. He knew that in that condition he couldn't expect anything from the Lord.[8]

It reminded him of Peter. When Peter saw Jesus walking on the sea, he said, "Lord if it's You, tell me to come to You on the water." Jesus replied, "Come!"; so Peter got down from the boat and walked on the water toward Jesus. But when he felt the wind and how strong it was, he panicked, lost courage and began to sink.

When Ted felt the burden of the lack of finances and the days slipping away until they had to pay their daughter's tuition, he too felt like he was "beginning to sink." Then he remembered that when Peter became frightened and began to sink, he cried out for the Lord to save him, and immediately Jesus stretched out His hand and took hold of Peter. Peter had begun to doubt when he took his eyes off Jesus and His command to "come," and looked at and felt the threatening wind and waves.[9]

It was time for Ted and Mary to put their faith in who God was and in His word to them. The issue wasn't whether or not they had faith in their faith. The issue was if they had confidence in the One who had promised provision for them. God, the faithful and loving One, supplied their need through friends and a second job.

After He came down from the Mt. of Transfiguration, a man ran up to Jesus and, kneeling down, asked the Lord to have mercy on his son because of a demon that oftentimes tried to destroy the boy. The man had brought him to Jesus' disciples but they weren't able to cure the child. He pleaded with Jesus, "If there is anything that You can do, have pity on us and help us." Jesus responded, "If You can? All things are possible to him who believes." Immediately the boy's father cried out, "I do believe. Help my unbelief!" Once again, Jesus stresses that everything is possible for the one who has faith. The boy's father did have faith, but he wanted help where his faith was falling short.[10] How often do we find ourselves with the same lack of faith because we are either unwilling to commit ourselves to the Lord or respond positively to His word?

When Jesus saw that a crowd was rapidly gathering, He rebuked the demon and it came out of the child who was instantly cured.

Afterwards, when they had gone indoors, the disciples came to Jesus and asked why they couldn't cast the demon out. Jesus said, "Because of the littleness of your faith." They had little trust.

Well, how much faith did they need? "Truly, I say to you, if you have faith the size of a mustard seed, you will say to this mountain, 'Move from here to there,' and it will move; and nothing will be impossible to you" (Mt. 17:20). How often does the poverty of faith affect our Christian life?

Jed and Melissa have three children and a dog named Skipper. Jed is a loving husband and a good father. He has been faithfully putting money aside ever since their wedding day. Yet Jed has always been anxious about supplying his family's needs: what they could afford to eat, what clothes the family would need next, and how much more money he needed to save in order to have the security and riches he longed for.

For Jed, life consisted of food, clothing, and work. He felt like his life was in suspense, and he wavered between hope and fear, especially since his company had been laying people off for the past three years. All these things disturbed him greatly. Jed hardly ever mentioned anything to his wife but she knew how worried he was.

One day Melissa sat down with Jed and had a talk with him. She asked him if he thought that God wanted him to continue to focus on amassing more and more money and to continually be anxious about his family's needs. "After all," she said, "don't you think life means more than food and money, and a person's body is more important than clothes?" (Sounds like she had been reading the Scriptures!)

The following Sunday the minister read Jesus' words from Matthew 6:26-33. As Jed later pondered over the text and message, he began to see things in a different light. He knew that he and his family were more precious to his heavenly Father than any bird, and yet He continually took good care of the birds. It also made sense to him that if God had so beautifully adorned the grass that is green today but tomorrow is dry and thrown into the fire, He is much more ready and likely to clothe his family. How little he truly trusted God! He needed to stop worrying and he had to quit asking "What are we going to eat today?" Or, "What are we going to wear tomorrow?" With his present attitude, he was running after all these things just like his non-Christian friends were. His heavenly Father knew that he and his family needed things. He began to see that his security could never be found in accumulated wealth.

Jesus had it right. Jed needed to set his heart on God's kingdom and the righteousness that is required. He needed to begin believing that all these "other things" would come to him and his family as a matter of course. His heavenly Father knew what they needed. Jed had to quit fretting over tomorrow and let tomorrow take care of itself. Every day did have enough trouble of its own.

The change didn't happen overnight, but as Jed meditated on Jesus' words and the Father's character, change did occur. Whenever he would begin to fret or be bothered about finances, he would quickly say, "No! I am not going to worry!" Then he would tell God every detail of his needs in earnest and thankful prayer. Jed cast every worry and concern that he had upon the Lord because he knew that God was concerned for him and would take care of him. He found that God's peace, which transcended all the powers of his thought-life, guarded his heart and mind.[12]

For Personal Reflection/Group Discussion:

1. How do the Scriptures describe "faith"? Describe it in your own words or pictures.

2. Discuss Jed and Melissa and their doubts, and how they became "believers."

3. What are some of the things you worry about and how does it relate to your faith (or lack thereof)?

4. Discuss the statement: Faith is logical, being based on evidence, and is not a blind leap in the dark.

5. Discuss the "fine line" between trusting God to supply

all your needs and thus doing nothing and pursuing that which you need. For instance, if you have a job that barely supplies what you need, is the answer to simply "have faith" that God will take care of you, or should you actively pursue another job by reading the want ads and applying for other/better employment?

REFERENCE NOTES TO CHAPTER TWELVE

[1] Larson, Craig Brian, *Choice Contemporary Stories & Illustrations for Preachers, Teachers, & Writers,* Grand Rapids: Baker Books, 1998 as written by Ramon Williams in the *Christian Reader,* pg. 284.

[2] Rom.3:28; 5:1; Gal.2:16; 3:8, 26; Rom.3:25a; Acts 26:18, 15:9.

[3] II Cor.1:24; Rom.11:20; II Cor.5:7; Heb.11:4, 7-9, 30.

[4] Heb.11:6.

[5] Heb.11:1, 11.

[6] Rom.1:17; Acts 18:8, 8:9-12; Heb.4:2.

[7] Mt.21:19-20.

[8] Cf. Ja.1:6-9.

[9] Mt.14:29-30.

[10] Mk.9:22b, 23, 24b.

[11] Mt.17:20. Even though Jesus also told them that that kind of demon could not be driven out by anything but prayer (Mk.9:29), the importance of faith cannot be denied. See, Mk.11:23-24.

[12] Cf. Phil.4:6-7; I Pe.5:7.

Chapter 13

Pressing On, Pressing On

He was a powerful man of God. Talk about revelation! He got it—so many times. His background was that of a legalistic know-it-all who hated Christians. On one occasion he took care of the clothing of those who were stoning to death a Christian named Steven. Thankfully, he eventually got saved. But it was no 'typical' conversion.

Still uttering murderous threats against the Lord's disciples, this man went to the high priest and asked him for letters addressed to the Jewish congregations at Damascus. He wanted to put these people in chains and take them as prisoners to Jerusalem. While on his journey, as he was nearing Damascus, a light from the sky suddenly flashed all around him and he became blind. He fell to the ground and heard a voice saying, "Saul, Saul, why are you persecuting Me" (Acts 9:4)? Saul wanted to know who it was, and the voice said, "I am Jesus, whom you are persecuting. Arise, go into the city and it will be told you what to do" (Acts 9:5-6). Imagine if you had been one of Saul's traveling companions! They stood there speechless, hearing the sound of a voice but seeing no one. Saul got up from the ground and they led him into Damascus. Later Ananias came to him and Saul received back his sight.

Saul, later called Paul, was soon proclaiming Christ publicly and eventually suffered and endured many things for Christ's sake. As he grew more vigorous and powerful, people became astonished.

This same man wrote most of the epistles in the New Testament. What is so remarkable is that for all the personal experiences and revelations that the apostle Paul had, he never had any greater goal than to know Christ. This was still his aim in life thirty years after his conversion and after having written I & II Corinthians, Galatians, I & II Thessalonians, and the book of Romans! Paul eagerly pressed on to know Jesus and continued to grow in grace and become better acquainted with his Lord.[1]

In the book of Hosea, God speaks of Israel as having broken their agreement with Him and having betrayed Him. Their goodness and love "vanish[ed] like morning clouds." God dealt severely with them. Whether out of sincerity and true repentance or just out of the desire to get back into God's good graces, Israel expressed their hope that He would soon raise them up and set them on their feet again to live under His care. God truly desires that we eagerly strive to know Him, which echoes the cry of Israel, "Let us press on to know the Lord."[2]

"Thus says the Lord, 'Let not a wise man boast of his wisdom, and let not the mighty man boast of his might, let not the rich man boast of his riches; but let him who boasts boast of this, that he understands and knows Me, that I am the Lord who exercises lovingkindness, justice and righteousness on earth; for I delight in these things,' declares the Lord" (Jer.9:23-24). God's delight is that we understand and know Him.

How do we get to know the Lord better and more personally? I remember when I came to the Lord over 35 years ago. I wanted to get to know Him and His Word more deeply. As time passed, I got the idea that I should get up in the morning to pray and read the Scriptures. That didn't sound like the best idea since I was used to doing most of my activities in the evening. The thought persisted. I decided to wake up five or ten minutes earlier and spend that time with the Lord. After doing it for a day or two, I began to think that I needed more time. I started to spend 15 minutes in the morning before the Lord. That only lasted a day or two and I felt that I still needed more time, and this continued until I was spending a lot of time in the mornings before the Lord—because I wanted to, not because I "had to."

The point is: when you are trying to get to know someone better and more deeply, you develop the desire to spend more time with that person—alone. Besides that, there is also the question of the quality of time that is spent together.

Grace and Matt had been dating for a few months. They had previously been going out with friends, but now they wanted to spend that precious time with each other. It didn't take long for Grace to see that her relationship with Matt was going nowhere. She confronted him and he was totally surprised. He thought that their relationship was going great. They liked a lot of the same things. In fact, they'd spend their weekends going to football games or other sports events. During the week they would go to a movie, hang out and fix his car or go out with friends. They were together a lot. However the problem was that they hardly ever talked about anything of substance. Most of their conversations were spent talking about what city or country had the best soccer team, which friends they liked, what their favorite foods were, and what was wrong with their college.

Matt was very interested in Grace and was even thinking of marrying her someday. Yet how much did they really know about each other? They knew some things that the other liked to do, which friends they both had in common, and what their favorite foods were, but they had no idea about each other's home background, their other likes and dislikes, their expectations of each other and Matt had no idea about what a healthy relationship consisted of. That they needed to begin discussing some deeper issues with each other just didn't make any sense to him. To Matt's frustration and Grace's sadness, a few months later their relationship ended.

Knowing God isn't about what prayers we can get Him to answer for us, nor is it simply intellectually studying about Him in the Scriptures. There needs to be a progressive and experiential knowledge of Him firsthand. This is what Matt couldn't understand regarding his relationship with Grace. She wanted a relationship that went beyond knowing who Matt's favorite soccer team was or what kind of ice cream he liked the best.

What things does God delight in? What kind of relationship does He want to have with you? It would also be good to ask yourself, "What kind of relationship do you presently have with God?" And, "how much do you really know Him?"

When my wife, Milta, and I went to live in Brazil many years ago, with our 3 and 5-year-old daughters, I carried with me a "slight" doubt regarding God's faithfulness. The doubt wasn't very big—I thought—so why would it ever give me any trouble? Interestingly enough, whenever a need arose or a crisis happened, that "slight" doubt would always take center stage. I tried to believe that God was completely faithful, and I talked to Him about my "difficulty."

It wasn't until a number of months later when Milta and I went to a conference in São Paulo that hope was instilled in me regarding this problem. A speaker gave the suggestion that we choose an attribute or quality of God and find out how God exercised it in the Scriptures. I definitely liked that idea. I decided to study and reflect on all the Scriptures in the Old and New Testaments regarding God's faithfulness. I looked at two or three verses each day during my devotions. I read one, wrote it out, and studied it. By the time three or four months had passed, I was totally convinced that God was (and is) faithful in all of His doings. It wasn't simply head knowledge. Those times I spent getting to know God gave me the opportunity to see how He acted and felt in different circumstances and how He was always faithful in them.

Actively meditating on the Scriptures as you seek to know and understand God on a deeper level is the key. Remember that meditation is not sitting still, keeping one's mind thoughtless and empty, and trusting that God will fill it with His words. It involves fixing one's mind on the Word of God, actively reflecting upon it and pondering it as we trust the Holy Spirit for help in understanding and applying the Word. As the Scriptures enter your heart you can meet and experience the living God.

Wayne Grudem writes, "All that Scripture says about God… is in a broad sense spoken of in human terms or in terms of the creation we know. This… is the way that God has chosen to reveal Himself to us, and to reveal Himself truly and accurately… Each description of one of God's attributes must be understood in the light of everything else that Scripture tells us about God. If we fail to remember this, we will inevitably understand God's character wrongly.

"For example, we have an idea of love from human experience… but our understanding of the meaning of 'love' when applied to God is not identical with our experience of love in human relationships. So we must learn from observing how God acts in all of Scripture and from the other attributes of God that are given in Scripture, as well as from our own real-life experiences of God's love, if we are to refine our idea of God's love in an appropriate way and avoid misunderstanding."[3]

Perhaps there is something that is not clear to you about God. Maybe there is a character quality of His that you need to understand much better in order to apply it in your life, as well as deepen your relationship with Him. Perhaps it has to do with God's mercy, love, grace, compassion, glory, goodness, holiness, justice, patience, power, immutability (the fact that He never changes), etc. Look up the quality in a concordance and begin to study and meditate on that attribute, asking the Lord to help you understand Him better and have a closer relationship with Him.

Here are some other ideas (and prayers) for your consideration in "pressing on to know the Lord":

- "First of all, since You are the Lord, please give me a heart to know You and understand You better and more deeply." (Cf. Jer.24:7)

- "You showed Israel Your acts and what You could do. But You revealed Your ways and intentions to Moses. (Ps.103:7). Teach me to know Your ways, O God, and not just Your acts, great as they are."

- "Make me fully able to comprehend and to know for myself the dimensions of Your love for me. I know that You can do this because You are able to do far more than anything that I can ask or ever dream of through Your power that works in me. (Cf. Eph.3:19-20)

- Ask the Lord to show you how to seek Him more actively and how to press on to know Him more intimately.

- Give the Lord time to express His heart to you as you read His Word and actively meditate on it.

- Express your admiration, love and delight in the Lord and thank Him for Himself as well as for His care, nearness, support, comfort, fellowship and sustenance.

- "Show me, O Lord, more of the beauty of Your person and Your uniqueness."

- "You're my best Friend. Show me how to be one of Your best and closest friends."

Will you "press on to know the Lord"? Are you committed to do this through His grace and help? As you follow on to know Him, He will give you the zeal to obey Him and to understand Him more deeply. It's by His Spirit that you will come to appreciate and cherish more and more who He is. That is His will for you and me.

Do you remember the purpose of the apostle Paul even after having been converted for thirty years? He tells us in Philippians that he was determined to know Christ, to experience the power outflowing from His resurrection, and to know what it meant to share with Him in His sufferings.[4]

Hopefully this book has helped you to focus in on these goals and to press on in your Christian life. We began by asking if a life pleasing to the Lord can be lived here on earth or if it's just a goal to try to reach. We've seen that it is possible to live a life that is thoroughly pleasing to the Lord. We saw that as a new creation in Christ our relationship with sin as master, with the law and with the world has ceased by what Jesus did on Calvary. We know that it is only the Holy Spirit who can make these facts a real experience in our lives by the grace of God. However there is still a life to be lived. We must deal with temptation—God's way. We know the principles needed to discern the will of God, and how to live victoriously in this world with its suffering. We know the importance of keeping a clear conscience, of abiding in Christ, of living a life of faith and of continuing to press on to know Him. Push through whatever would try to hinder you. And may our Lord continue to give us wisdom, knowledge, understanding, discernment and grace as we walk on in the victory and freedom that He has provided in Christ.

For Personal Reflection/Group Discussion:

1. Reflect/discuss what it really means to know someone and how to get to know them better. How would you apply those ideas and principles in getting to know the Lord better? What else can be done to press on to know Him?

2. Discuss Wayne Grudem's observations.

3. Name at least four things you can do in the next 30 days to get to know the Lord more intimately. Choose one of these each week.

4. Thinking through all that you have read in this book, how are you going to be different when you put this book down than when you first picked it up?

REFERENCE NOTES TO CHAPTER THIRTEEN

[1] Cf. Hos.6:3; cf. II Pe.3:18.

[2] Hosea 6:7, 4b, Taylor; Hosea 6:3.

[3] Grudem, Wayne. *Systematic Theology.* Grand Rapids, MI, Zondervan Publishing House. 1994. Pgs.158-159. Used by permission of Zondervan.

[4] Phil.3:10.